Liberalism and the Free Society in 2021

by Brad Lips

ATLAS NETWORK

Liberalism and the Free Society in 2021

By Brad Lips
Edited by Lisa Conyers and Dara Ekanger
Cover Photograph by Jeremy Bishop on www.unsplash.com
Latin America Photographs by Rodrigo Abd
Asia and Europe Photographs by Bernat Parera
North America Photographs by Isaac Torres
Book and Cover Design by Colleen Cummings

ISBN: 978-1-7325873-1-1
Ebook ISBN: 978-1-7325873-2-8
Library of Congress Control Number: 2021909935

Atlas Network
Two Liberty Center
4075 Wilson Blvd.
Suite 310
Arlington, VA 22203
www.atlasnetwork.org

Liberalism and the Free Society in 2021

Table of Contents

Introduction The Meaning of 2020 Depends on What Happens Next 7

Section 1 – A Movement Centered on Freedom and Dignity 11

1. The State of the Freedom Movement in 2021 12
2. Great Achievements of the Liberty Movement Over Forty Years 20
3. A Freedom Movement Centered on Human Dignity 26

Section 2 – The State of Liberalism and the Free Society in 2021 49

4. The Fragile Foundations of Our Free Societies 50
5. Findings from the 2021 Global Index of Economic Mentality 54
6. Land of the Free, Home of the Brave? 59
7. Avoiding a New Lost Decade in Latin America 78
8. Is This the Asian Century? 94
9. A Wider Overton Window for the Sick Men of Europe 109
10. Africa at the Dawn of Its Continental Free Trade Area 125
11. A Decade Since the Arab Spring 140

Section 3 – A Path Forward for Liberalism and the Free Society 159

12. A Path Forward..160

Thank You...179
About the Author..180
About Atlas Network... 181

Introduction
The Meaning of 2020 Depends on What Happens Next

1776. 1848. 1917. 1989.

There are certain years in which the course of history has taken a sharp turn, sometimes for better and sometimes for worse.

Have we just lived through one in 2020?

Have the restrictions that were imposed to address COVID-19 brought us to a "new normal" that's left us less free than before?

It may take years to answer this question; just as the full meanings of 1776 and 1917 were not immediately obvious. It is not preordained that the future should be less free, less safe, or less prosperous than the course we were on in 2019. There are countless alternative futures that seem very plausible from my vantage point as this book goes to print in June 2021. Which one we will live in is very much up in the air.

What do you believe about the future of liberalism? Is it a rising or setting sun on the cover of this book?

If you are like me, you are hopeful that we are, in fact, at the dawn of a new era for the free society. In this scenario, the future will see not just the survival of liberal democracy but its flourishing.

It will be a future that offers dignity, economic opportunity, and legal equality to all people.

A future in which our most vexing problems are solved through bottom-up experimentation of countless innovators.

A future that does away with the government-granted "privileges" that, I'm convinced, will one day seem as anachronistic as titles of nobility.

Perhaps you're not just rooting for this future but are actively working for it and investing in it. If so, this book—an assessment of the state of *Liberalism[1] and the Free Society in 2021*—has been written with you in mind.

My target audience is primarily composed of participants in what we call the "freedom movement." They are people who believe freedom is both a noble end in itself and also the essential catalyst for producing other important outcomes: peace, prosperity, tolerance, and cultural enrichment among them. People in the freedom movement understand that, while there may be a time and place for partisan politics, our energies and resources can have greater impact by advancing and popularizing classical liberal *principles.* Many in this movement devote their careers or their philanthropy to organizations that collaborate with Atlas Network, where I have worked since 1998 and have been CEO since 2009.

---

1 "Liberalism" is a term that has been misused in some parts of the world, especially the United States. At the end of this Introduction, I explain why I suggest reclaiming its original meaning.

Of course, I'm hopeful that this book will reach not just my kindred spirits inside the freedom movement but a broader audience as well. Let's call them the "liberty-curious." These are people who might put a different label on their ideology, or no label at all, but who are sufficiently concerned about the direction of society that they want to explore new perspectives for insight.

If I have just described you, dear reader, thank you for taking genuine interest in how new ideas and new coalitions might ward off threats to the free society and help more regular people achieve their dreams.

The book is organized in three parts:

Section 1 looks at the past and present of the organized freedom movement.

The occasion of Atlas Network's fortieth anniversary makes this an opportune time to look at advances of freedom in recent decades that have been cheered on—and, as you'll see, often helped along—by visionary partners of Atlas Network.

In this section, I make observations about the state of the freedom movement based on proprietary information that I have collected from Atlas Network's partners and allies.

I put a special spotlight on innovative recent work by Atlas Network partners—documented in this volume with some really gorgeous photojournalism—that conveys how freedom and dignity are liberalism's common denominators.

Section 2 sizes up the state of liberalism and the free society worldwide, using a variety of indices that measure freedom and the institutions that sustain it.

Among them, there is a new research project that I am proud to have helped develop: the Global Index of Economic Mentality (GIEM). The GIEM gauges public sentiment about the appropriate role of government in economic matters. I am hopeful that, as the GIEM is further refined, it will prove helpful in identifying countries that are vulnerable to declines in economic freedom or ready for advances.

The remainder of Section 2 consists of fascinating conversations that I was privileged to convene with civil society leaders in six regions of the world. These chapters—on Africa, Asia, Europe, Latin America, the Middle East and North Africa, and the United States and Canada—offer insight and perspective on the state of our world as seen through the eyes of principled classical liberal scholars, reformers, and activists.

Finally, Section 3 presents "A Path Forward."

These are my suggestions for how the freedom movement and its allies might focus efforts to achieve more impact in the years ahead.

I offer suggestions knowing that there's not a *single* best path forward, but that all of us in the freedom movement should be intentional in how we direct our efforts. All of us should listen to newcomers with open minds as we navigate a litany of complex challenges.

Whether you browse this book or read it cover to cover, you'll come to appreciate that the countries of the world have some common challenges and some unique ones.

○ Can we find a path back to economic dynamism after the COVID-19 lockdowns, without calamitous health consequences from this or any subsequent pandemic?
○ Can we build more resilient societies so that more of humanity's full creativity and innovativeness can be applied to other Black Swan-type disruptions?
○ Can we remove the cancer of cronyism that privileges the few at the expense of the many?
○ Can we reduce the political polarization that is fueled by identity politics from both the Left and the Right?
○ Can we rekindle appreciation for free speech and genuine pluralism during an era of cancel culture and agenda-driven media?
○ Can we demonstrate that liberal democracy is, in fact, superior to the illiberal regimes that stifle individualism in order to pursue nationalist ends?
○ Can we regain momentum in putting an end to extreme poverty?

Making headway on these challenges, and more, is the task of our freedom movement.

I hope we'll be proud of our progress—not in dismay over what we've lost—when Atlas Network celebrates its fiftieth anniversary in 2031.

A Note on Embracing "Liberalism"

The term "liberalism" has been abused through the years, but this seems the right time to rehabilitate it and embrace it.

In this book, the term is used to describe the institutional framework that protects individual rights and offers equality under the law. This is how liberalism is understood in much of the world, outside the United States.

In the United States, classical liberal values are embedded in our nation's Founding documents and treasured along different parts of the ideological spectrum, including by many "conservatives" who see American Exceptionalism deriving from the embrace of individual liberty.

In recent years, however, parts of the conservative movement in the United States have pushed away from this classical liberal tradition. Simultaneously, the more radical part of the center-left coalition which once—very confusingly—self-identified as liberal, now marches under the banner of "progressivism." The polarization that exists between these loud, illiberal extremes on the left and right of our political spectrum presents many problems. But the upside is that it leaves more of us feeling disaffected with the two major parties and yearning to re-establish a commonsense center to American politics.

My hope is that a wide array of Americans can rediscover "liberalism" and embrace its true spirit—respecting the dignity of the individual, celebrating pluralism in society, modeling tolerance and civility, and demanding that government stay in its proper lane so the voluntary sectors of society are empowered to solve most problems.

Across the world, we can prove also that our principles ought not to be dismissed with the slur "neo-liberalism," as happens in Latin America and some other regions. Yes, it is appropriate to criticize the cronyism that festered amid liberal reforms in many countries after the fall of the Berlin Wall. But it is inappropriate to throw out the liberal project because of these violations against it. It is up to us in the freedom movement to make this case and correct these misperceptions.

We need to go on offense to show what I know is in our hearts: that authentic liberalism is at odds with any system of political privilege, and is the best hope for all those who seek true equality under the law.

Brad Lips
June 3, 2021
Arlington, Virginia

SECTION 1

A Movement Centered on
Freedom and Dignity

Chapter One
The State of the Freedom Movement in 2021

The future is full of opportunities and challenges that we glimpse but do not fully comprehend. Our understanding of the future is—by necessity—grounded in our understanding of the present. Too often, this limits our imagination about the possibilities in front of us.

History remembers those who anticipate opportunities for change and celebrates those who bring positive changes into reality. The legendary venture capitalist Peter Thiel—hunting for the mix of courage, vision, and contrarian thinking that marks the best entrepreneurs—likes to ask, "What important truth do very few people agree with you on?"

I have three answers to that question:

1. Most people today are pessimistic about liberal democracy; the truth is that illiberal coalitions are unstable, and the principles of freedom are poised for a revitalization across the world.
2. Most people today think the ideological debate is won and lost in political campaigns; the truth is that the climate of ideas is really shaped through education and civil society.
3. Most people are not even aware of the "think-tank community" that makes up much of the freedom movement described in this chapter. Those who are tend to think this community is out of touch, resting in ivory towers with little connection to practical problems. The truth is that, at their best, think tanks can have an outsized impact on the opportunities enjoyed by regular people.

My big hypothesis is that a great deal of history will unfold in the 2020s, and the groups that make up the freedom movement are undervalued assets for revitalizing liberal democracy and ensuring a brighter future.

While our Atlas Network team has no pretensions that we "define" the freedom movement or are its single hub, we do engage in a meaningful way with a significant number of classical liberal organizations around the world known as our global network of independent partners. This puts us in a special position to draw upon the proprietary information we collect from our partner universe to make observations about the state of the freedom movement.

175
US & Canada

103
Latin America

125
*Europe &
Central Asia*

10
*Middle East &
North Africa*

25
Africa

As of May 2021, Atlas Network has 479 independent partners in 97 countries that, if combined, would have an aggregate annual budget estimated at $1.05 billion.

34
*Asia
& Pacific*

7
*Australia &
New Zealand*

"If you want to go fast, go alone. If you want to go far, go together.

This saying has been mislabeled as an African proverb on thousands of web pages, but even if we don't know where it originated, it is still full of wisdom.

Our liberal cause needs a sense of solidarity if we are to be more successful in extending the benefits of free societies to more of the world's population. Each person involved with the promotion of human liberty can find ideas and inspiration from like-minded peers in their own regions and around the world. Is this happening?

In February 2021, some 259 people who work for independent partners of Atlas Network opted in to a survey I designed to discover: Are we really even a "movement"? To what extent are our spirits buoyed through bonds of friendship and shared purpose? Or have the challenges of the COVID era sapped our spirits?

I was grateful to discover an abundance of happy warriors in my survey's results, although I am mindful that there is much room for improvement in the levels of connectedness and collaboration among our partners.

Finding #1—When asked, "To what degree do you get satisfaction from your work in the freedom movement?" **86 percent** expressed very high or high satisfaction.

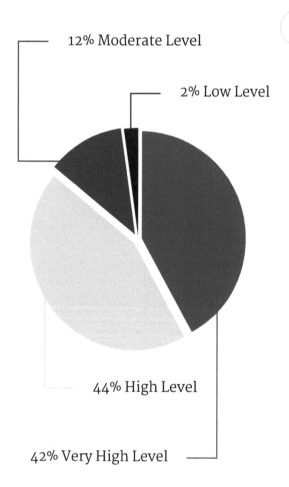

12% Moderate Level

2% Low Level

44% High Level

42% Very High Level

Finding #2—**42 percent** of the respondents feel highly connected to the global freedom movement, but this percentage increases to 54 percent if you isolate the sample that have attended Atlas Network's annual conference for the global liberty movement, the Liberty Forum and Freedom Dinner.

Finding #3—**52 percent** feel highly connected to the freedom movement in their region, but this goes up to 60 percent among the cohort that have attended in-person trainings of Atlas Network with their peers.

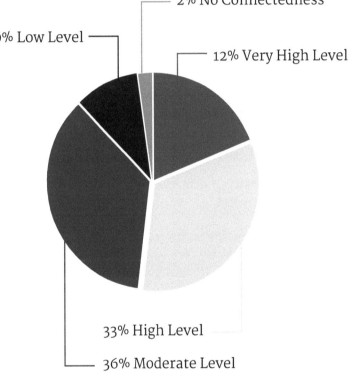

2% No Connectedness

10% Low Level

12% Very High Level

33% High Level

36% Moderate Level

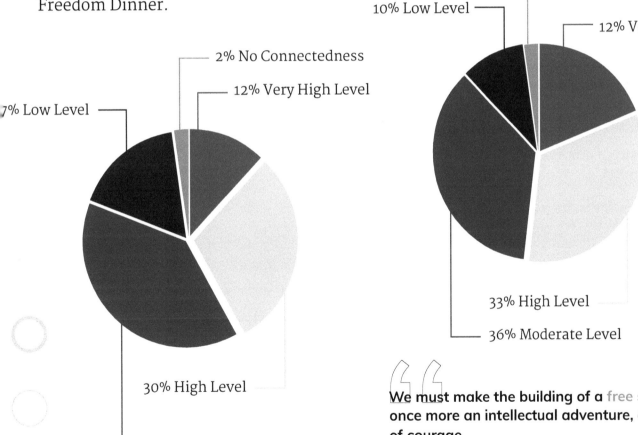

2% No Connectedness

12% Very High Level

7% Low Level

30% High Level

39% Moderate Level

> **We must make the building of a** free society **once more an intellectual adventure, a deed of courage.**
>
> —FA Hayek, *The Intellectuals and Socialism* (1949)

While there is a great deal of diversity among the organizations that partner with Atlas Network, this page provides a rough profile of a typical partner, using the median budget among our sample and other proprietary data that our team collects on the players in the liberty movement.

When Atlas Network's founder, Sir Antony Fisher, encountered skepticism that a modestly staffed, sparsely funded think tank could influence the direction of a country, he would explain that each group had a part to play, and indeed a multitude of them could change the climate of ideas. To make his point, he used to cite a bit of schoolbook poetry from his youth in Britain:

> *What if the little rain should say, "So small a drop as I,*
>
> *Could ne'er refresh a drooping earth, I'll tarry in the sky"?*

The median budget of Atlas Network partners is

$280,000

More than 70% of Atlas Network partners were founded after the year 2000

The average Atlas Network partner has seven full-time staff members.

Age of Atlas Network Partner Organizations

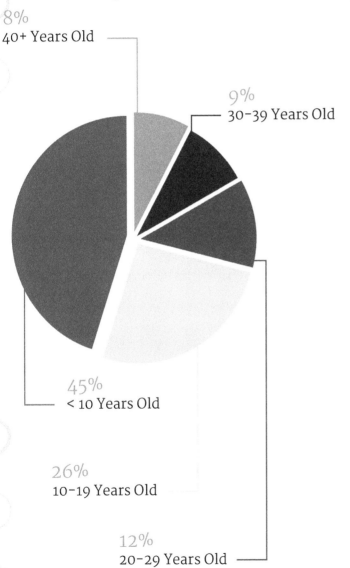

8%
40+ Years Old

9%
30–39 Years Old

45%
< 10 Years Old

26%
10–19 Years Old

12%
20–29 Years Old

As an organization Atlas Network refuses to accept financial support from government as a matter of principle. For the most part, our independent partners have adopted the same stance. Only four percent of funding comes from government or quasi-government entities funded by taxpayers.

Sources of Funding

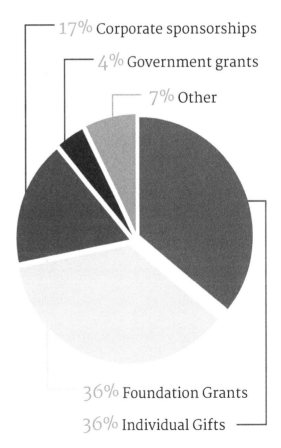

17% Corporate sponsorships

4% Government grants

7% Other

36% Foundation Grants

36% Individual Gifts

Participants in my February 2021 survey were challenged to think about how organizations in the freedom movement need to improve to have a greater positive impact on societies.

The Top Ten Identified Needs Were:

1. Greater sophistication in messaging and marketing
2. More engagement with audiences that don't yet see the common ground they share with classical liberals
3. Growing new funding sources
4. More collaboration between organizations in the freedom movement
5. More programming for reaching youth audiences
6. Attracting and retaining leadership talent to drive new innovation and success
7. More sophistication in government relations so ideas are implemented in reform
8. More focus on practical policies vs. abstract ideas
9. Avoiding partisans or illiberal ideologues who might appear as allies for a fleeting policy win, but who could cause lasting damage to the reputation of the freedom movement
10. Creating our own media platforms to transcend the problems

Survey participants also were asked to identify up to three pressing challenges for the freedom movement in the year ahead, and then three topics that are likely to increase in importance over the coming decade. I took the liberty of grouping common answers—knowing, of course, that tensions exist in how some respondents would want to address topics raised, like migration and climate change—to create these top ten lists.

The Freedom Movement's Immediate Challenges

1. Creating an economic rebound from the pandemic via economic freedom
2. Protecting free expression from new threats
3. Safeguarding civil liberties in an era of expanded government
4. Saving the rule of law from corruption, illiberalism, and identity politics
5. Climate change and energy policies
6. Decreasing poverty and improving social mobility
7. Inflationary risks related to increased government indebtedness
8. Improving educational options
9. Improving health care quality and access
10. Solving migration challenges

Big Topics for the Decade Ahead

1. Unsustainable levels of public debt and the financial crises that may ensue
2. Socialism's appeal among younger generations who have not experienced it
3. Cancel culture and Big Tech undermining free expression
4. Forms of identity politics that sacrifice individual rights to group rights
5. New technology frontiers (e.g., artificial intelligence and blockchain)
6. Appeal of authoritarian governance models
7. Climate change
8. Challenges relating to freedom of mobility and assimilation of immigrants
9. Decreasing poverty and improving social mobility
10. Protecting individual privacy

Many of these challenges, and others, are discussed in the regional conversations that make up the bulk of Section 2 of this book. Readers will be heartened, I expect, by the thoughtfulness with which classical liberals around the world are stepping up to the problems of our age, which are large and complex, but not without solutions.

The remaining chapters of Section 1 tour the progress that's been made on many fronts by liberal thinkers and free-market think tanks over the past forty years, as well as recent and ongoing work to extend greater freedom and opportunity to more people.

While there is certainly much room for improvement and innovation within the freedom movement as it exists in 2021, I am fully convinced that this community of independent voices can provide great leverage for saving and extending liberal principles in the years and decades ahead.

Chapter Two

Great Achievements of the Liberty Movement Over Forty Years

In Ron Manners's Toast to Freedom at our 2020 Freedom Dinner, he asked if we could imagine a world *without* Atlas Network and its nearly five hundred partners that strive to bring greater freedom and opportunity to populations all over the globe. "Terrible," he said. "What a terrible world that would be." Thankfully, this movement *does* exist and has continued to bring about notable positive changes.

This sampling of ten great achievements over forty years should be a source of inspiration. The world is a better place thanks to our network. As our movement grows and becomes more innovative, just think what can be achieved in the decades to come.

Privatization Instead of Nationalization

The privatization of British Telecom (announced July 1982), and other companies formerly owned and run by the UK government (e.g., Jaguar, Cable & Wireless, British Aerospace, Britoil and British Gas), was fueled by a Thatcher government that had been persuaded by work on this topic by think tanks such as the Institute of Economic Affairs, Centre for Policy Studies, and Adam Smith Institute. The co-founder of Adam Smith Institute, Eamonn Butler, puts this achievement in perspective:

"This was the biggest transfer of ownership—in this case from the bureaucracy to private citizens—since Henry VIII dissolved the monasteries in 1536."

Thatcher set the standard for transparent transformations of public firms that were monopolistic tax-consumers—propped up by a weak private economy—to tax-paying, profitable enterprises that are part of a robust and competitive private economy. A major lesson from the experience is the importance of the rule of law so that "privatization" does not become shorthand for shifting assets—or even worse, monopolies—into the hands of apparatchiks and cronies.

Property Rights for the Poor

Hernando de Soto met with Atlas Network founder Antony Fisher in 1980 to discuss plans for the Instituto Libertad y Democracia in Peru. Seven years later (1987), *The Other Path*, coauthored by De Soto with Enrique Ghersi, presented a recipe for inclusive prosperity in Peru. The book earned Instituto Libertad y Democracia the first-ever Fisher Award, an Atlas Network prize-program that ran from 1990 to 2016. Notably, De Soto's offices were bombed in 1992 by Shining Path terrorists who recognized how profoundly his work undermined their violent revolution. By the end of the decade, the World Bank and other establishment organizations had been persuaded by De Soto's vision of empowering the poor by getting their properties titled and their businesses registered. That revolution in practice inspired many more . . . in Ivory Coast, India, South Africa, the Philippines, and many other countries.

In building property rights on the secure foundation of the rule of law, Atlas Network partners understand that cadastral maps in a distant government ministry do not always reflect authentic reality. Our partners have been guided instead by the idea of "listening to the dogs"—that the law should reflect common understandings, which are even intuited by barking dogs that will let people know if they trespass on their owner's property. And this movement to establish legal property rights has liberated millions of rural people from harmful paternalistic restrictions and encumbrances on their titles; in the Philippines alone, 2.5 million "agricultural patents"—non-transferable titles of little value—were transformed into full property thanks to the patient and meticulous work of the Foundation for Economic Freedom.

Undoing Communism

In the Soviet Union and the Communist Bloc, the underground circles that read and discussed liberal thought were often initiated by the professors of "bourgeois economic theory," who were allowed to read classical liberal economic works, the better to refute it. Unsurprisingly, after being exposed to the alternative, many abandoned Marxist dogma in favor of economic science and liberty. Tom Palmer, now with Atlas Network, met one such young professor from Prague at a celebration of F. A. Hayek's birthday at the Viennese Chamber of Commerce. That meeting resulted in Palmer's lectures and meetings in Prague, the smuggling of books in Czech, German, and English, and the formation of the F. A. Hayek Klub in Prague in 1989, followed by the Liberal Institute in February of 1990. One of their first projects was the translation of Paul Heyne's influential introduction to economics, *The Economic Way of Thinking*, which replaced the Marxist theology texts.

Other groups were established across the region as they struggled to break free from communism, and many of them also translated and published Heyne's book as an alternative to the Marxism still taught in schools. Palmer recalls, "A pivotal moment for the liberal community in East Europe came with the Cato Institute's first conference in the USSR in 1990, which was supported also by Atlas Network and for which I did advance work. [Former Cato President] Ed Crane deserves a lot of credit for putting resources where it counted, getting liberal books behind the Iron Curtain, and—let's not forget—pioneering the promotion of classical liberalism in China, notably through their 1988 conference at which Milton Friedman was treated like a rock star, surrounded by excited Chinese students. While Marxism is still an intellectual force, it no longer has a monopoly."

Sweden Embraces Economic Freedom

In the imagination of many, Sweden stands out as a working example of socialism. The history of the country, however, teaches a different lesson. Sweden had lagged behind the rest of Europe in economic growth for a quarter century before its historic policy reforms of the early 1990s—reforms that took inspiration from the early research of Timbro Foundation, one of Sweden's leading think tanks and a long-term Atlas Network partner. In fact, the founder of Timbro hired two researchers in the early 1980s who both went on to become leaders of major political parties during the reform era.

In the 1990s, labor markets were made more flexible, taxes were cut, limits were placed on government spending, and market competition was brought to education and health care. While the Swedish government continues to preserve a large safety net for its citizens, it learned that economic growth and free competition is the way to afford and ensure high quality within the benefits it provides.

Helping to End Apartheid in South Africa

When Apartheid was dismantled in the early 1990s, South Africa's classical liberals could take pride in having steadfastly opposed the evil system of segregation since before its imposition on society. The South African Institute of Race Relations (IRR) was estab- lished in 1929 to support cooperation among different groups in South Africa to oppose apartheid and other forms of legal inequal- ity. They campaigned for equality of rights and organized scholarships ("bursaries") for students, including Nelson Mandela, who re- ceived IRR support to complete his legal stud- ies in 1947. Today they continue to "fight for your right to make decisions about your life, family, and business, free from unnecessary government, political, and bureaucratic in- terference."

IRR was joined in 1975 by the Free Market Foundation, which also campaigned against the "guild socialism" of Apartheid and worked to instill a love of equal liberty and the principles of liberalism among all popula- tions, notably through bestselling books such as *After Apartheid*, by Leon Louw and Frances Kendall, and by sponsoring American econo- mist Walter Williams, author of the 1982 book *The State Against Blacks*, to lecture and speak in South Africa, which resulted in his influential work *South Africa's War against Capitalism*.

Such organizations share credit for leading South Africa toward restoration of property rights for all South Africans, including the majority who were dispos- sessed by the Native Land Act of 1913 and subsequent acts of theft. Along with newer partners, such as the Centre for Develop- ment and Enterprise, these organizations are steadfastly working for a free and open South Africa, based on equal rights for all.

Measuring Economic Freedom

One of the most influential ideas in modern political economy—using metrics to spur competition among nations to excel at economic freedom—was born from a debate at a Mont Pelerin Society meeting in 1984. Fraser Institute's founding president, Michael Walker, recalls, "I was invited to comment on Paul Johnston's paper, titled '1984, A False Alarm?' And while I agreed that Orwell's vision of an omni-intrusive state had not materialized, I took the position that there had been a significant loss of economic freedom in many countries. Milton and Rose Friedman were among those who were frustrated by the lack of a common vocabulary about how to judge the level of economic freedom across countries. This led to a series of six Liberty Fund colloquia, organized by the Fraser Institute, which produced several new approaches to the topic and finally the prototype *Economic Freedom of the World Index*, produced by James Gwartney, Robert Lawson, and Walter Block, which was released in 1996."

Other organizations joined Fraser Institute in this research space, including The Heritage Foundation (*The Index of Economic Freedom*, published with *The Wall Street Journal*) and The World Bank (*Doing Business* report). Sub-national indices (measuring economic freedom in provinces or states) have been constructed for the United States, Canada, Mexico, Germany, and even mainland China. Atlas Network partners have engaged Fraser's research team to conduct "Economic Freedom Audits"—spurring substantial media coverage of market reform ideas—in more than a dozen countries including Brazil, Ghana, Greece, Kyrgyzstan, Tunisia, and Vietnam.

Achieving Monetary Stability Where There Had Been Hyperinflation

Much of Latin America suffered serious hyperinflation in the 1980s, eroding living standards of many already living in poverty. Ecuador was in such a situation in the year 2000 when its government made the decision to withdraw its own national currency, ending its central bank's ability to print money and leading to a new era of price stability.

Atlas Network's Rómulo López—born in Guayaquil, Ecuador—reminisces, "The hero of dollarization was Dora de Ampuero, who led the Instituto Ecuatoriano de Economía Política and who popularized this solution among other free-market figures in the country, Romulo Lopez Sabando, Joyce de Ginatta, and Franklin Lopez Buenaño. Dollarization was criticized by the likes of Joseph Stiglitz and Jeffrey Sachs, but Dora had allies in economist Kurt Schuler and Atlas Network's then CEO Alejandro Chafuen, among others in the region focused on sound money. A key theme was that dollarization stopped the impoverishing of the most vulnerable; the upper class always had ways to shift assets to other currencies, but working Ecuadorians had received *sucres* that declined in value as they ran to spend them, before they became worthless. The success of dollarization showed sound money serves the needs of the poor, and despite political instability in Ecuador and socialist governments in the last twenty years after its implementation, the only thing that brought stability and some sense of normalcy was dollarization."

The Rise of Pro-Liberty Public Interest Litigation

While most of Atlas Network's partners defend the principles of free societies in the court of public opinion, some defend the liberties of specific individuals in court. Groups like Institute for Justice, Pacific Legal Foundation, and Goldwater Institute have won significant legal victories and established important precedents to curb the discretionary power of government. John Kramer, vice president of communications at the Institute for Justice, remarks: "There has never been a better time in modern American history to bring an economic liberty case than now, and I look at IJ's victory in the *Saint Joseph Abbey* case as an important tipping point."

The case at hand saw the State Board of Embalmers and Funeral Directors move to shut down the selling of homemade wooden caskets by the monks of a Benedictine monastery in Covington, Louisiana. The monks and IJ won a landmark decision in federal court to establish that courts can strike down laws that arbitrarily violate the right to earn a living. The *Abbey* decision became the framework for other appeals in federal and state courts, creating a new dialogue about how the courts should think about economic rights.

Co-Creation to Accelerate Freedom

Manuel Ayau and the other co-founders of Guatemala's Universidad Francisco Marroquín were far-sighted in 1) creating a governance model that would sustain a high-quality experiment in higher education, and 2) imbuing the university with a culture of innovation. One innovation, driven by the late Giancarlo Ibárgüen, was the Antigua Forum, founded in 2011 to disrupt the typical conference model favored by think tanks and academia.

"Giancarlo recognized that the typical conference is too often a waste of time and talent, and run in a way that's inconsistent with our principles," explains Antigua Forum Executive Director Wayne Leighton. "This is because smart people are forced to only listen with no way to marshal the dispersed knowledge in the room. Most productive engagements are pushed to the coffee breaks, where spontaneous interactions foster creativity, networking, and offers to collaborate.

Giancarlo conceived of the Antigua Forum as a purposefully structured ongoing coffee break with a mix of entrepreneurs, policy reformers, nonprofit leaders, investors, and academics. This co-creation event has a few rules of engagement—like a market economy—where everyone is laser focused on sharpening projects to have real impact, seeking first to understand their challenges and then developing practical solutions to overcome them."

The Antigua Forum has helped influential projects around the world, from trade policy to charter cities, from education to health care. The effectiveness of the Antigua Forum's co-creation process has inspired others in the freedom movement to adopt it for their events. The Antigua Forum has also commissioned practical, instructive case studies in how policy reforms took shape in New Zealand in the 1980s, in the Guatemalan telecommunications industry in the 1990s, and in the Republic of Georgia following the Rose Revolution in the first decade of this century.

Changing the Narrative on Foreign Aid
Acton Institute received the 2015 Templeton Freedom Award for its documentary film, *Poverty Inc.* The film won more than sixty international film festival awards and was praised from all parts of the political spectrum. Documentarian Michael Moore commented, "You'll never look at poverty and the Third World the same again."

The film, at once heartfelt and thoughtful, contributed to an intellectual shift away from the government-to-government aid schemes that peaked around the ONE campaign in 2004. Distributed on Netflix and Amazon Prime, the documentary provided inspiration—for one of the first times since the late Bob Chitester's *Free To Choose* PBS documentary with Milton Friedman—that a liberty-oriented film could have a major impact on new audiences.

While certainly not an exhaustive list of the accomplishments and innovations that have been aided and celebrated by organizations in the liberty movement, this chapter hopefully serves as a reminder that we can achieve big breakthroughs.

An important take-away is that all of these accomplishments happened over years of patient work. Friends of the free society may find it frustrating that there are no shortcuts to momentous moments like the fall of the Berlin Wall, but I am convinced we improve the odds of watershed victories for liberty only by sticking to the work at hand—that is, explaining why freedom works, and taking thoughtful, consistent action toward authentic liberal reforms that will improve the lives of regular people.

Chapter Three
A Freedom Movement Centered on Human Dignity

Liberalism and the free society face headwinds in 2021 from both the populist right and the collectivist left.

Those on the extreme left won't accept at face value that we sincerely believe free enterprise is an engine of opportunity for all. They prefer to mischaracterize our efforts as a racket for protecting the interests of the wealthy.

Those on the extreme right dismiss us as globalists who threaten their communities' traditional values. They reject our hypothesis that issues of sovereignty can be reconciled with our belief that all people deserve dignity and opportunity.

While I think these critiques are unfair, we need to take them to heart. There are reasons why the populists feel anger toward the elite that created concentrations of political, economic, and cultural power.

If they conflate our vision of free societies with the schemes of Brussels bureaucrats and Washington insiders, it suggests we have not done enough to explain our belief that strong free societies are built from the bottom up. If they see us as pawns of billionaires, we clearly have failed to draw the line between the entrepreneurial capitalism we favor and the crony capitalism we despise.

For our freedom movement, the path forward needs to be centered on human dignity.

I am excited that 2022 will see the release of what promises to be an important book with the working title *Development with Dignity: Self-Determination and the End to Poverty*, co-authored by my Atlas Network colleagues Matt Warner and Tom Palmer. Warner and Palmer make the compelling case that economic development, the ostensible aim of our failed foreign aid model, is best advanced by local voices who understand the crucial roles of human dignity and the liberal institutions that protect individual freedoms.

In their forthcoming book, Warner and Palmer amass strong evidence, highlighting the work of many of our partners, to show that by trusting individuals to use their local knowledge to improve their own situations, societies can become more prosperous and more resilient to face difficult crises in the future.

Of course, there are many important audiences that are unlikely to pick up a book on this topic at all. That reality has motivated Atlas Network and its peers in the freedom movement to work on improving our storytelling around the human beneficiaries of the policy changes we favor.

To that end I am delighted to present the following photojournalism pieces, commissioned on four continents over the past three years by Atlas Network—working with Pulitzer Prize-winning photojournalist Rodrigo Abd in Latin America, Bernat Parera in Asia and Europe, and Isaac Torres in the United States. They help us show that liberal policy reforms enhance the well-being of real people in communities all over the globe.

ASIA

When Ram Chandra Mahato returned to his home town of Biratnagar, Nepal, after a stint working as migrant laborer abroad, he purchased an electric-powered rickshaw and began plying his trade. When city authorities decided to regulate the rapidly growing industry, they capped the number of driving permits at three hundred. This left over thirteen hundred drivers, including Ram, out of a legal way to make a living.

Bikalpa (meaning "an alternative"), a Nepalese partner of Atlas Network, stepped in to work toward the removal of the cap alongside other civil society groups to create public pressure for change via protests, newspaper editorials, and policy advocacy in the media. Basanta Adhikari, Bikalpa's founding chairperson, explained why it is important that Nepal welcome entrepreneurs, rather than incentiv- izing them to emigrate, "No one wants to be away from their home country. For any country, economic freedom is extremely important. Until there is economic freedom, the holistic growth of an individual is not possible."

Today Ram and his family enjoy the benefits of having him home and gainfully self-employed without fear of government penalty.

ASIA

Dinesh and other millions of street vendors in India—who answer to regional names such as hawkers, pheriwala, rehri-patri walla, footpath dukandars, sidewalk traders— were all at the mercy of the police before the Protection of Livelihood and Regulation of Street Vending Act was passed in 2014.

This law secures the rights of street vendors and fosters a congenial environment for urban vendors to ply their trade without harassment or eviction by the local authorities. The legislation also establishes Town Vending Committees that look into matters affecting street vendors. The Centre for Civil Society, an Atlas Network partner based in India, was instrumental in advancing this groundbreaking legislation, which helps street vendors like Dinesh have a voice in the system, and it continues to monitor and report on the legislation's implementation.

Today, Dinesh is an elected member of one such Town Vending Committee in New Delhi—and is happy with his newfound freedom to ply his trade in peace.

ASIA

In rural Nepal, Lorik Prasad obtained a bank loan to start a tractor-mounted mobile mill business. He now drives his tractor from house to house, customer to customer, providing a much-needed service to his rural community. His neighbors no longer have to transport their grains for miles to get to the closest mill.

The Samriddhi Foundation, an Atlas Network partner based in Nepal, is working to ensure vague, outdated business regulations aren't used by special interests to quash innovations like Lorik's that improve the lives of everyday people.

"Thirty million Nepalis like Lorik are being deprived of economic freedom," said Akash Shrestha, Samriddhi's research coordinator. "Our mission is to enable the people of Nepal to use their own talents to improve their own living standards and contribute to a more prosperous society."

EUROPE

Viktor Tsytsyura owned a 3.5-hectare parcel of fertile farmland in Ukraine, but was too old to farm it, could not sell it, nor use it as collateral in a bank loan. This was the reality for roughly seven million Ukrainian landowners who, after the collapse of the USSR, received 32 million hectares in plots of land from their government as compensation for years of toil on collective farms.

When the Ukrainian government awarded the land in the aftermath of communism, it also introduced a "one-year" moratorium on selling that land. Nineteen years later, that moratorium was still in place.

EasyBusiness, the Kyiv-based think tank, along with The Ukrainian Economic Freedoms Foundation, the Centre for Economic Strategy, and Ukrainian Students for Freedom—all Atlas Network partners—did extensive and important work on the issue of land reform for many years, and in 2020 the moratorium was repealed, with the establishment of a market to follow in mid-2021. Viktor is now free to sell the land he owns, as are millions of other Ukrainian landowners.

EUROPE

Ona Raudeliūnienė is a skilled baker of *šakotis*, a traditional Lithuanian holiday cake, which she sells thanks to a simple government business license that allows people with full- or part-time jobs to dabble in running a small business. Today, about one hundred thousand Lithuanians take advantage of these licenses, but the threat of losing this tool is very real.

The pernicious attempts to end this license program take many forms, from limiting which professions are covered to trying to abolish the program entirely. Licenses for business owners in childcare, automotive repair, and construction services are no longer available and fees for others have been raised.

Atlas Network's partner, The Lithuanian Free Market Institute (LFMI) is often a lone voice in defense of the licenses. Says Aneta Vainė, vice president of LFMI, "People like Ona operate simple businesses that people need and like. . . .We should make it easy for such people to work and supplement their income."

LATIN AMERICA

In Costa Rica, Luis Diego Soto Clausen has been perfecting his craft—creating delicious nougat candies—for more than thirty years. When he was ready to expand his factory, he ran into burdensome roadblocks. That's when he turned to the **Instituto de Desarrollo Empresarial y Acción Social** (IDEAS), a San José-based free-market think tank and Atlas Network partner.

Luis Loría and his team at IDEAS worked with the Ministry of Economics, Industry, and Commerce (MEIC) to design and implement policies to help small businessmen like Soto have greater access to credit—and thus more opportunity to build their businesses. In the wake of these changes, Luis Diego was able to expand his factory and employ more workers.

Luis's *Turrones Doré* nougat candy is now available in more than 450 stores across Costa Rica, Mexico, Guatemala, Nicaragua, Dominican Republic, and Puerto Rico.

LATIN AMERICA

Libertad y Progreso, an Atlas Network partner in Argentina, created a media campaign that led to the elimination of a standing 35 percent tariff on laptop computers and small electronics that made these products very expensive compared to prices in neighboring countries.

This one trade policy reform made it possible for a local cooperative, La Juanita, to purchase new computers and help students build skills that could lead to greater job opportunities.

Agustín Etchebarne, the general director of Libertad y Progreso, knew that lowering the tariff would have a powerful impact on people who were struggling to make a living.

"Many people believe that public policy that makes computers cheaper is an abstract achievement. But there is nothing abstract about creating new jobs for poor people."

LATIN AMERICA

Verónica Canales wanted to open a small hardware store in Lima, Peru, but found the onerous tax code too hard to overcome. José Ignacio Beteta, president of the Lima-based Asociación de Contribuyentes del Perú, a taxpayer watchdog organization, took on her cause and the cause of thousands of other small entrepreneurs.

"Working with the Peruvian government's tax agency, José and his team designed changes to the tax code so that small-business owners like Veronica could flourish. With their help, the Peruvian government decided to let business owners pay their taxes *after* they received payment for their products, rather than before.

As a result, Veronica now has a thriving store in the Mercado Mayorista.

USA

Truth Graf went from PTA president to a prison cell. A series of stressful and traumatic events culminated in Truth's drug addiction, and she spent seven years in prison. Truth is now a passionate volunteer advocate for criminal justice reform. Atlas Network's partner the Georgia Center for Opportunity is one of the local nonprofits that helps the formerly incarcerated like Truth find employment.

The Georgia Center for Opportunity works with Truth and others like her to help bridge the gaps between recovery and community reintegration, and they work with local companies ready to hire the formerly incarcerated.

Georgia once had the worst incarceration rate in the country, with one in thirteen adults being under some form of correctional supervision, but after a concerted effort by the state—in partnership with organizations such as Georgia Center for Opportunity—that number is now one in nineteen and is trending in a positive direction.

USA

West Virginia's education system had terrible test scores, high dropout rates, and by most measures was simply lagging behind. Despite spending more than the national average per student, the state's education system provided no flexibility and was failing its students.

Atlas Network's partner the Cardinal Institute was instrumental in the state's 2019 decision to allow the establishment of charter schools for the first time, and in 2021 it celebrated West Virginia's new Hope Scholarship program, which will give 90 percent of West Virginia students access to educational savings accounts tailored to their needs. Cardinal continues to work to increase the flexibility that parents and students have available to them.

A great example is Jennifer White, who homeschools her three sons. Her oldest struggled in public school after he was not given the tailored approach his dyslexia required. She now tutors public, private, and homeschool students with dyslexia. She identified a shortcoming—a market gap—and filled it to provide a service that works for students in need.

What I love about the stories in this chapter is that they show the enterprising spirit of people from all over the globe. Bad policy has blocked them from opportunities, but they found allies in Atlas Network partners. Changing bad policy helps not just the protagonists of these stories but millions more in similar circumstances.

The lesson I take is that our understanding of the old aphorism about giving a man a fish is incomplete. Indeed, direct aid is a short-term strategy, appropriate for an emergency, but not practical for the long term. But "teaching a man to fish" misses the point too. Most people acquire useful skills on their own, without needing any outsider to tell them what to do.

The real challenge in most poor communities is a lack of legal or economic rights.

When free society institutions are in place, you discover that the poor are perfectly capable of taking care of themselves and creating (to stick with our fish-centric metaphor) fisheries or other productive enterprises that create benefits for the broader community.

Our freedom movement can help create the environment in which people can use their own capacities and choose their own destinies. We reject the patronizing paternalism of so many elites who presume to know how others should live their lives. We instead bring to the table a genuine respect for each person's dignity and agency, confident that this will be the engine of new social progress.

SECTION 2

The State of Liberalism and
the Free Society in 2021

Chapter Four

The Fragile Foundations of
Our Free Societies

The median age of the 7.7 billion people on planet earth is thirty-one years old, which means more than half of humanity was not even born when the Berlin Wall fell in 1989. It is no wonder that the triumphalism that existed among advocates of market liberalism has softened over time, as fewer people have memories of its Cold War alternative.

The world has become increasingly prosperous over this time span, including during the last decade between the 2008 global financial crisis and the current COVID-19 pandemic. That's the obvious conclusion from the Legatum Institute's *2020 Prosperity Index*, which noted that the 2010s saw rising incomes, better education, and improved living conditions across all regions. However, the foundations of our prosperity could be lost with the fading memories of the lessons of socialism's failure in the Soviet Union.

The report *Freedom in the World 2020*, an annual publication of Freedom House, shows that—for the fourteenth consecutive year—more countries have declined than improved in Freedom House's measure of freedom.

The authors single out for special concern not only China and its Communist Party's detention and forced indoctrination of millions of Uighurs in Xinjiang, but also India where the ruling Bharatiya Janata Party stokes a Hindu nationalism that undercuts the country's commitment to individual rights. Freedom House's authors also note that populists in Europe and the Americas have been tempted toward similar rhetoric—and, in some cases, action—to marginalize minorities within their borders in order to shore up political power.

To date, the declines we see in measures of political freedom have not been matched by declines in measures of economic freedom. On a global scale, economic freedom has continued to move in a positive direction, though not at the heady pace of the 1980s and 1990s. The *Economic Freedom of the World* report saw the global average of the 123 nations in its survey increase their economic freedom score to a score of 6.98 in 2018 from 6.63 in 2000, approximately one third of a standard deviation over this period.

It is notable, however, that one of the component pieces of the Index has barely budged at all over this time: that being the rule of law. This reflects how the political class is able to game the rules in so many countries, siphoning off an unjust percentage of the wealth gains that should accrue to economic actors across society.

It is tragic that the free enterprise system—with all its successes in lifting living standards—is despised by so many because they, very understandably, conflate it with cronyism. The daily wonders of entrepreneurial capitalism, improving access to quality goods while lowering prices through competition, are almost invisible next to the shocking excesses that come from an alliance of big business and big government. No wonder the 2019 Edelman Trust Report, a massive survey of worldwide opinion, found a majority (56 percent) agrees with the statement: "Capitalism as it exists today does more harm than good in the world."

Another dispiriting trend lies in the dashed hope that increasing economic liberty in autocratic countries would foster liberal democratic reforms. China was to be the great case study. When British rule of Hong Kong ended with the Hand Over of 1997, it seemed reasonable to hope that China would continue to become more like Hong Kong. The opposite has transpired, and now we will see whether Hong Kong—consistently topping indices of economic freedom for as far back as we have data—will see its economic dynamism diminished in the wake of blows to its political autonomy.

Hong Kong's great media entrepreneur Jimmy Lai now languishes in jail, along with many other pro-democracy dissidents. At Atlas Network's Liberty Forum in November 2020, Lai predicted the island would decline as a financial industry hub:

> Hong Kong now—with its rule of law and freedom [being chipped] away—I don't think its status [as a] financial center will still work. Because in the financial business, billions of dollars are transacted in a second; without mutual trust this is not possible. And mutual trust is only possible if we have rule of law and freedom.

Because the rule of law has remained weak in many places, the benefits of economic growth have not been as widely shared as hoped. Yes, huge numbers have escaped extreme poverty and even greater percentages have seen meaningful improvements in their circumstances, but the game appears to be rigged.

No wonder we see a boiling over of resentments against elite insiders. This begs the question: will economic institutions be sustainable if they're seen as benefiting the few instead of the many?

The riots that erupted in late 2019 in Santiago, Chile, were startling for many of us who previously had celebrated the country as an exemplar of economic freedom. Evidence showed that Chile's gains were widely shared. Extreme poverty as defined by the World Bank fell in Chile from 34.5 percent to 2.5 percent between 1990 and 2015, and the middle class expanded over the same period by 24 percent to reach 64 percent of the population. Income inequality fell, social mobility improved, and Chile led all Latin American countries in the 2019 UN Human Development Index.

Opponents of Chile's liberal economic regime pointed to how pro-market reforms had been put in place by the dictator Augusto Pinochet. But this is a non sequitur. We can despise the human rights abuses of the Pinochet era while acknowledging that the free-market policies implemented by his economic advisors proved beneficial to Chilean society and especially the poor. On the basis of the economic track record, Chile seemed to most an unlikely place for a hard left insurrection.

But not everyone was surprised by this turn of events. Axel Kaiser, now a fellow with Atlas Network's Center for Latin America, wrote in 2007 how Chile's economic success had not translated into a public consensus about economic freedom. "Chile is heading toward failure," Kaiser wrote. "The end result will be the return of the Latin American mediocrity that characterized our history prior to the free-market reforms made by the Chicago Boys [economists associated with the University of Chicago who advised on economic reforms in Chile]." At some point, we could even see the breakdown of social peace and soldiers occupying the streets again" (*El Chile que Viene* by Axel Kaiser).

Similarly, Professor Carlos Newland of Argentina has noted that Chile has appeared consistently among the lowest-ranked countries in terms of appreciating the institutions of economic freedom, according to the World Values Surveys taken in recent decades.

Newland invited me to join him and his co-author, Pál Czeglédi, in formalizing research on this topic as the "Global Index of Economic Mentality (GIEM)," which will be presented formally in the fall 2021 issue of the *Cato Journal*.

The GIEM offers at least a preliminary empirical tool for assessing economic attitudes and causal beliefs about markets and the appropriate role of government. This is a research agenda that responds to

the insights of thought leaders like Nobel Prize-winning economist Douglass North; the Russian-born historian Alexander Gerschenkron; and the founder of modern business strategy theory, Michael Porter. These three were interested in how cultural norms and popular attitudes could explain why some countries prospered and others did not.

More recently, in her "Bourgeois Era" trilogy, economic historian Deirdre McCloskey makes the case that the incredible increase in wealth after the Industrial Revolution cannot be explained satisfactorily without looking at the role of ideas and rhetoric. It might seem our modern world can be explained simply as the results of new markets and new innovations, but other points in history did not see lasting prosperity come from similar discoveries. What was unique to the Great Enrichment (her term) of the nineteenth and twentieth centuries was the shift in opinion about private property, commerce, and middle-class lifestyles. What had been disparaged for millennia was being treated approvingly. Thus, the wealth of nations grew so dramatically because economic factors were supported by moral ones; rhetoric about markets and free enterprise finally became enthusiastic and encouraging of their inherent dignity.

With McCloskey's insights in mind, we might consider what we would find in a future iteration of the *Economic Freedom of the*

World report—in say, 2031 or 2041—if more of the world came to appreciate the wonders of free enterprise.

Conversely, it's easy to imagine a more dystopian world, with vastly less freedom in the economic sphere, if the socialists and the nationalists succeed in their attacks on free and open markets.

We can look to the GIEM for ideas about which way we might be headed.

Chapter Five
Findings from the 2021 Global Index of Economic Mentality[2]

The Global Index of Economic Mentality (GIEM) measures the extent to which people value private initiative, free competition, and personal responsibility over greater government intervention, income redistribution, and a supportive government.

Based on statistical analysis of data from the World Values Survey, the GIEM uses three variables:

o *Efficiency*—the extent to which people believe private ownership and competition between firms produces desirable economic results;
o *Redistribution*—the extent to which people are in favor of a redistributive state; and
o *Responsibility*—the extent to which people believe that the individual is responsible for his or her own well-being, as contrasted with a view that the government should directly take action against poverty and in favor of income equality.

At this point, we have data to include seventy-nine countries in the GIEM rankings. Unfortunately, the sample omits some significant countries such as India, South Africa, and Canada, and only includes a few countries in Africa. Nevertheless, the available data allows for some interesting findings.

First, we do find that there is a strong correlation between economic freedom and GIEM scores. We cannot make any empirical claims about causality, but it is striking that many of the countries that score highest in the GIEM do enjoy relatively high levels of economic freedom, and a similar association exists at the bottom of the scale.

Of course, within the country scores, there lies additional complexity. For instance, while New Zealand ranked first in the overall GIEM scale, it fell only in the middle of the pack on the GIEM's sub-indicator concerning "personal responsibility," showing a lingering sense that the government does have a role to play in insuring its citizens' overall wellbeing.

While there is a general association between economic freedom and economic mentality, it is interesting to look at outliers. These may be countries that are primed for economic reform in the direction of freer markets, despite currently low levels of economic freedom; or they may be prone to backsliding, despite relatively free institutions today.

Figure 1 lists countries whose divergence from the mean GIEM score is stronger than its divergence from the mean in the *Economic*

2 This chapter presents summary findings of a paper I co-authored with Pál Czeglédi (associate professor at the University of Debrecen in Hungary) and Carlos Newland (professor of economic history at ESEADE University and Torcuato Di Tella University in Argentina). "The Economic Mentality of Nations" is scheduled to appear in the forthcoming edition of *Cato Journal*, Vol. 41, No. 3 (Fall 2021).

GIEM RANK	COUNTRY	GIEM SCORE	EFW RANK*
1	New Zealand	0.75	3
2	Czechia	0.743	25
3	Sweden	0.718	46
4	United States	0.704	6
5	Bulgaria	0.655	32
6	Georgia	0.65	8
7	Romania	0.65	23
8	Denmark	0.643	11
9	Poland	0.637	77
10	Australia	0.636	5
11	Estonia	0.625	14
12	Armenia	0.624	18
13	Albania	0.622	26
14	Slovenia	0.609	62
15	Belarus	0.603	114
16	Great Britain	0.596	13
17	Colombia	0.594	92
18	Taiwan	0.591	16
19	Guatemala	0.587	35
20	Vietnam	0.585	125
21	Malaysia	0.578	46
22	Switzerland	0.573	4
23	Hong Kong	0.564	1
24	Hungary	0.556	53
25	Portugal	0.551	43

GIEM RANK	COUNTRY	GIEM SCORE	EFW RANK*
26	France	0.545	58
27	Brazil	0.531	105
28	Nicaragua	0.529	74
29	Norway	0.523	43
30	N. Macedonia	0.515	71
31	Mexico	0.514	68
32	Japan	0.51	20
33	Slovakia	0.506	38
34	Germany	0.506	21
35	Netherlands	0.505	24
36	Peru	0.505	29
37	Ethiopia	0.501	146
38	Austria	0.495	26
39	Jordan	0.487	39
40	Finland	0.483	29
41	Serbia	0.481	74
42	Iceland	0.476	34
43	Ecuador	0.473	110
44	Thailand	0.465	88
45	Kyrgyzstan	0.463	78
46	Croatia	0.458	61
47	Lithuania	0.457	11
48	Nigeria	0.451	81
49	Cyprus	0.448	22
50	South Korea	0.428	36

GIEM RANK	COUNTRY	GIEM SCORE	EFW RANK*
51	China	0.426	124
52	Philippines	0.425	54
53	Greece	0.417	92
54	Italy	0.416	51
55	Bolivia	0.409	116
56	Zimbabwe	0.397	155
57	Iraq	0.392	146
58	Kazakhstan	0.39	73
59	Lebanon	0.39	83
60	Tajikistan	0.367	132
61	Pakistan	0.35	129
62	Turkey	0.347	99
63	Spain	0.344	33
64	Argentina	0.343	144
65	Chile	0.34	14
66	Indonesia	0.327	59
67	Tunisia	0.324	129
68	Iran	0.318	158
69	Egypt	0.313	152
70	Azerbaijan	0.313	112
71	Russia	0.31	89
72	Montenegro	0.297	80
73	Bangladesh	0.266	133
74	Ukraine	0.264	131
75	Myanmar	0.261	142
76	Bosnia	0.231	82

*out of 162

Figure 1

Freedom of the World report. Some of these countries are pretty high in both rankings, but Vietnam, Belarus, Ethiopia, Colombia, and Ethiopia stand out as belonging to the EFW's bottom two quartiles today. These countries could be poised for positive change.

1. Czechia (EFW Rank: 25)
2. Sweden (EFW Rank: 46)
3. New Zealand (EFW Rank: 3)
4. Vietnam (EFW Rank: 125)
5. Belarus (EFW Rank: 114)
6. Poland (EFW Rank: 77)
7. United States (EFW Rank: 6)
8. Colombia (EFW Rank: 92)
9. Bulgaria (EFW Rank: 32)
10. Ethiopia (EFW Rank: 146)

On the other hand, the above shows countries with GIEM scores below where one might expect given their existing position in the *Economic Freedom of the World* report. As discussed in the previous chapter, Chile stands out as especially vulnerable to falling from its current lofty position in the EFW, but this list also includes Spain, Indonesia, and Montenegro, which currently place in the top two quartiles of the report.

1. Bosnia (EFW Rank: 82)
2. Chile (EFW Rank: 14)
3. Spain (EFW Rank: 33)
4. Indonesia (EFW Rank: 59)
5. Montenegro (EFW Rank: 80)
6. Ukraine (EFW Rank: 131)

7. Russia (EFW Rank: 89)
8. Bangladesh (EFW Rank: 133)
9. Myanmar (EFW Rank: 142)
10. Azerbaijan (EFW Rank: 112)

To facilitate global analysis, we grouped countries according to geographic categories: Australia and New Zealand, Europe, Latin America, East Asia and the Pacific, Sub-Saharan Africa, West Asia and North Africa, and Central and South Asia. With no available data from Canada at this point, and including Mexico with its Spanish- and Portuguese-speaking neighbors in Central and South America, we treat the United States as a standalone at this point.

United States (GIEM Score: 0.70): We found that in the United States people value private competition and do not prize income transfers. The scores are somewhat lower in the category of personal responsibility.

Australia and New Zealand (average GIEM Score: 0.70): The economic culture seems to be similar to the United States, with the population valuing private competition, not prizing income transfers, and scoring lower in the category of personal responsibility.

Europe (average GIEM Score: 0.51): Scores in this region were quite varied. Czechia, one of the most successful countries of post-communist Eastern Europe, ranked number two overall. Sweden, perhaps to the surprise of many who associate its welfare state with socialism, ranked number three in the GIEM. Perhaps it is fair to say that it is precisely the high level of economic freedom and mentality in Sweden that permits it to sustain a generous welfare state. Not all is rosy for economic mentality in Europe. The bottom of the GIEM scale finds Ukraine and Bosnia, countries that have had tumultuous histories since the break-up of the Soviet Union and communist Yugoslavia. GIEM scores tend to be higher in Northern Europe and lower in Southern Europe. Interestingly, several ex-communist countries in Eastern Europe present high GIEM values.

Latin America (average GIEM Score: 0.48): Colombia and Guatemala lead the region, while Argentina and Chile presented the lowest values. Although Latin America is one of the most unequal regions in the globe, income redistribution is not prioritized by its population to the extent that we see in other regions. At the same time, its countries score low in our measures of private initiative and competition.

East Asia (average GIEM Score: 0.47): This extraordinary and dynamic part of the globe is quite homogeneous in how it values the market economy. Two outliers exhibiting rather low scores are Indonesia and Myanmar, the latter being one of the least-free countries in the world with its recent history mostly dominated by dictatorship.

Sub-Saharan Africa (average GIEM Score: 0.45): Unfortunately, our data set consists only of Ethiopia, Nigeria, and Zimbabwe for this region. Its rankings fall in the lower-middle section of our overall GIEM.

North Africa and the Middle East (average GIEM Score: 0.43): This somewhat heterogeneous region, stretching into West Asia as far as Iran, found GIEM scores to be low across all variables, especially in the redistribution and responsibility categories.

Central and South Asia (average GIEM Score: 0.37): All variables were low, especially in the redistribution and efficiency categories.

Another interesting way to look at the GIEM data is through the lens of age. My coauthors and I divided the survey results into two, to see how GIEM scores would change if you looked only at results of the "under 40 years old" and "40 and over" cohorts.

In looking at the under-40 group, the ranking of countries is transformed in a rather surprising manner. Among the ten highest-scoring countries, seven are from Eastern Europe. Secondly, developed countries of Western Europe and the Anglosphere generally rank lower in this measure as compared with the overall GIEM. New Zealand, the number 1 country with the overall index, is now ranked number 3. Sweden falls from 3 to 10; the United States from 4 to 16; France from 27 to 34; and Germany from 36 to 52.

One possible explanation of this data suggests that there may be a natural "convergence of economic mentality," as younger people in an economically free society may tend to take for granted the benefits of a free enterprise and rebel against the beliefs of the older generation.

Readers in the United States will find it disconcerting, but perhaps not surprising, that there is no other country in our GIEM data set with as large a gap between the economic mentality of older and younger generations.[3] Survey data over recent years has consistently shown that American millennials (born 1981–1996) and members of Generation Z (born 1997–2012) are more favorable to socialism than capitalism.

Why is this? And is this phenomenon, while particularly acute in the United States, also a challenge in other parts of the world? These are questions that are picked up in the following chapters, as I convened wide-ranging discussions of issues that threaten free societies across six major regions of the world.

---

3 The lone exception is the country of Estonia, except the scores run in the opposite direction, with the younger cohort much more favorable to free enterprise than the older.

Chapter Six

Land of the Free, Home of the Brave?

The United States of America as well as its northern neighbor, Canada, historically have been viewed as examples of successful free societies—worthy of the grandiose closing lines of "The Star Spangled Banner." But are Americans still living in "the land of the free and the home of the brave" in 2021? Does Canada still represent "The True North, strong and free"? How do we regain what seems to have been lost? Where do we find, and how do we address, the root problems that now stress the foundations of these liberal democracies?

In early April 2021, I discussed these questions with *Lindsay Craig* (executive director of National Review Institute); *James Otteson* (The John T. Ryan Jr. Professor of Business Ethics at the University of Notre Dame); *Avik Roy* (president of the Foundation for Research on Equal Opportunity); *Lenore Skenazy* (founder of the Free-Range Kids movement and now president of Let Grow); as well as the co-directors of Atlas Network's Center for North America, *John Tillman* (also, chairman of the Illinois Policy Institute) and *Niels Veldhuis* (president of the Fraser Institute in Canada).

Brad Lips

I'd like your thoughts on one of the more interesting findings within the Global Index of Economic Mentality project I've been working on. Of the seventy-nine countries in the study, measuring appreciation for free enterprise, the United States has the biggest generation gap. The "under 40" set in the US is much more favorable to big government. Why?

Jim Otteson

I'll make two broad observations based on my twenty years of being a professor. There has been a change in higher education that could be fueling this, which is a blurring of lines between scholarship and advocacy. Once upon a time, most professors across the political spectrum would have agreed that what went on in universities was scholarship. Policy advocacy and training happened in other places: foundations, think tanks, opinion journalism. Now, many don't recognize the distinction and may positively believe that all research should be in the service of the correct vision of the good life. Because most of academia leans left, that means in practice that their research aims to advance moral sensibilities that presume a big role for government. That may explain, to some extent, the left-leaning sensibilities that you're picking up on among younger adults, though it may not explain support for socialism in particular. I see a more complex phenomenon there.

Frankly, a lot of people under forty don't know what socialism is. They did not grow up with the Cold War, so it's often news to my students that some variant of socialism has been attempted on national scales in over two dozen countries over the last hundred years. They've had no idea that there are results of socialism to study. So their views are mostly based on simple associations; they think socialism means caring for the poor, helping those in need, not being selfish, and treating people fairly. Who could possibly be against those things? If you ask them "What is capitalism?" it means the opposite: ignoring people who are in need, selfishly grasping as much as you possibly can for yourself, and the rest of the world be damned. So if those are the alternatives on offer, it doesn't surprise me that a lot of people are going to support socialism.

Brad Lips

I'd like to get Niels's opinion here. We didn't have a data set to allow us to include Canada in the GIEM, so I'm curious if your intuition says Canada's young adults similarly are gravitating toward socialism?

Niels Veldhuis

Yes, this is a huge concern for us at Fraser Institute, which is why we have a pretty massive program coming forth on the myths and realities of socialism, because we see kids so attracted to this concept without even really understanding it in a historical context. To Jim's point, I agree that our education system has had a profound, negative impact, but I'd argue it stems all the way from K–12 schooling too. The education establishment has developed a curriculum that is against markets, that's antithetical to the development of natural resources. It's surprising how the social justice narrative is woven into just about every subject. In math class, I've seen the concept of ratios taught by showing how much more CEOs make than average workers without any context; the point seems to [be to] just ingrain a sense of unfairness into young kids who never get exposure to other ideas.

Another factor: I think of my own example, growing up in the Netherlands, shaped by what happened in Berlin. I was at the Berlin Wall before it came down. I was there again a year after it came down. Those were my defining years as a teenager. Young people today have grown up without this very clear tension between actual socialist and communist countries and the free societies they are blessed to live in.

Lindsay Craig

Yes, part of the reason these misunderstandings exist is simply that things are so good. Those of us in this discussion all understand that free enterprise and limited government are sources of human flourishing. But that message might not appeal to people who believe they can take for granted that there's plenty of food available, that almost everyone has air conditioning and can find ways to afford $180 sneakers if they really want. I've come to realize progressive politics are most accepted right now because things are actually so good, even in this pandemic.

Brad Lips

Yes, while lots of people have dealt with economic anxiety during the lockdowns, that's something different from deprivation. So perhaps a key takeaway is that, in an era of abundance, our graphs about economic growth trending with economic freedom are less persuasive. People are comfortable enough that they can focus on other perceived injustices—like others' opinions that they find "triggering." Lenore, I see a connection between this trend and the work you've been doing.

Lenore Skenazy

One of the things that I've noticed is that as things become safer, we become more obsessed with how unsafe they are. Abraham Lincoln had four children and only one of them made it to adulthood. Nobody said, "Wow, what a terrible dad he was! Why wasn't he paying attention?" Everyone back then understood how little control we have over our fates, so people were forgiving. "There but for the grace of God go I." Right?

Now, we can control more aspects of life, and it's caused parents to get this sort of "God complex," where we assume we can—and should—keep anything bad from ever happening to our kids. This is full of problems that have worked their way out into the culture.

For context, I should explain my story. When my kid was nine, I let him ride the subway alone, and I wrote a column about it in *The New York Sun*. Two days later, I was defending myself on *The Today Show*, MSNBC, Fox News, and NPR. I got the nickname "America's Worst Mom." You can Google it. After all the hoopla, I started a blog, and then I wrote a book called *Free-Range Kids* and then it became a movement, with the underlying message our kids are NOT in constant danger.

Now I run a non-profit called Let Grow, which I started with the help of Daniel Shuchman, who had been chairman of FIRE (Foundation for Individual Rights in Education), and Jon Haidt, who coauthored *The Coddling of the American Mind*. They saw universities dealing with students who were too fragile to wrestle with ideas they didn't already accept, so Jon and Dan said, "Hmm, the problem must be starting earlier, right? I think it's in our parenting culture and obsession with safety."

John Tillman
And let's point out that, with the pandemic, this pursuit of safety at all costs has gotten worse. I was listening to the old Jackson Browne song "Boulevard," on the way to work this morning, and the lyrics struck me as really relevant to what we're talking about.

Brad Lips
I'm sure we'd all love to have you belt out the song right now.

(Additional encouragement from others)

John Tillman
It goes, "Nobody rides for free / Nobody gets it like they want it to be / Nobody hands you any guarantee / Nobody." That's Jackson Browne in the '70s, and think about where we are

today. Everybody is owed something. Everybody looks to government for some guarantee of safety and well-being. The script has totally flipped!

Why is this? Well, it's the nature of government to need problems to justify their role. There's a great book, *Chasing the Scream*, by Johann Hari, that documents how the drug war traces back to a government bureaucrat in the 1930s who needs a new gig after Prohibition is repealed. There wasn't a huge drug culture to fight at the time, but there was enough for it to be a useful cause for ambitious people inside government. So, there you go, we get nearly a century of a growing and destructive drug war.

So when Lindsay points out that life in America is pretty damn good, the political class asks, "Well, what can be the new thing? What scream do we chase now?" The answer they have come up with is victimology.

The civil rights problem was largely solved in the 1960s—to the extent it could be solved by law; of course, healing human hearts is a longer process and one that can't be legislated. But ambitious activists in the civil rights space didn't just celebrate their victory and retire; they wanted more and cultivated this sense of victimology around minority status. Now we have victimology for everyone.

And one of the things I think we fail to really understand is how seductive victimology is to so many people and how destructive it is. With Americans this risk-averse, we never would have put a man on the moon. If something bad happens, we no longer understand it as happenstance or bad luck or part of the learning process; you must be the victim of some structure that's controlled by people of privilege who must be exploiting you.

That's the mindset. And once you get into it, focused on why terrible stuff has happened, it makes sense that the only proper arbiter of fairness, to properly allocate opportunity and equity, is the government. The government has to step in, because you've been victimized by this rapacious thing we call capitalism. That's how this all connects: the helicopter parenting, the seduction of socialism, and the willingness to take orders during the pandemic.

What's fascinating is that this mindset is being challenged right now. You see it in the breakdown between how Republican governors and Democrat governors are handling the late stages of the pandemic. Some (not all) Republican governors have leaned into their instincts to free things up and let people be responsible for their own decisions. The Democrat governors, by and large, have said the government will tell you how to be safe. We need to take care of you because one life at risk is too many.

Brad Lips

We can definitely be thankful for federalism, so we can learn from how different policies have played out in different states. By the same token, I expect we can learn lessons from our neighbor up north. Are there lessons Canadians learned in the course of the pandemic that the US should learn from?

Niels Veldhuis

Canada has had one of the greatest increases in government intervention in the developed world, and we have almost nothing to show for it. So one of the key lessons that comes from this, it seems, based on the emerging data, that the severity of lockdowns had almost no impact on the spread of COVID. A second lesson is to be careful about deference to experts whose expertise is very narrowly defined. It's surprising how public health experts don't take account of the unseen effects of their policies. It's exactly what Frederick Bastiat tried to teach us all nearly two hundred years ago! The damage of the restrictions has been significant—in the form of mental health, substance abuse, and in educational setbacks, particularly for kids at the lower end of the income distribution—and I imagine we will wonder in future years why these concerns were excluded from the cost-benefit analysis driving the lockdowns.

Lenore Skenazy

The lockdowns have worsened some of the family issues that I focus on—like the way kids today don't get to experience what we call "free play." Instead, we get adult-organized play where adults organize the teams and set the rules. And to some people it might look like play, but to me it looks like school that just happens to be teaching you soccer techniques. Adults think kicking the ball is the fun part, but the really important part of self-directed play is that the kids have to deal with each other, figure out the rules, figure out how to incorporate the little brother sometimes. These tasks are the beginning of developing executive function.

When you deprive kids of these opportunities, they get used to having someone else running their life. And so it doesn't surprise me that, after a couple generations of this, you have young adults who always expect somebody else to be mediating and solving the problems and making things fair, because they never got experience doing it.

Jim Otteson

That resonates with another change I've noticed over my career as a professor, which is the increasing number of students who come to me wanting me to solve various problems for them, as mundane as scheduling problems. "Wow, I have a test due on this day, and a paper in your class I have to write, and I'm in this club, and I don't know how I'm going to get it done." And now I've learned to just say, "Yeah, that sounds hard. Good luck with it." When I first started as a professor, I was much more willing and interested to talk with people and work through these problems. But now I just don't want to contribute to them being totally infantilized. They're nineteen or twenty years old, and they need to start to organize their own life.

Lindsay Craig

This discussion about what kids *aren't* learning also points to what I see as the biggest policy opportunity of the moment, which is in the education policy space. Parents during the pandemic have had an unprecedented exposure to how little of value their kids are learning in many schools. That presents a fantastic opportunity for the school choice movement and for pushing back against teachers unions that seem to have priorities very distinct from what parents prioritize.

People are seeing how private schools need to cater to what parents want. The public schools remain mostly closed where I live, but my daughter's private school has been in-person every day since September 15 because they know their customers would walk out on them if they didn't figure out how to make it work. The public schools serve parents who want the schools open, but those parents don't have any voice. And it's getting worse, as some of the public school districts are opting not to give the regular standardized tests this spring. Someone on the news this morning actually said, "This is not the year to test the children." Wow, right?

This is a terrible thing that's happened. Kids have been completely let down by the government's schools. But the upside is that the school choice movement has a window of opportunity to seize on public anger and show how there is a way to empower families to improve how their kids are educated.

John Tillman

That is a great issue. We need more fighting back and rebelling about what's not working, and it takes courage—especially in this environment concerning cancel culture and group identity politics. The key to fighting back successfully is having the back of people who show courage. Bill Maher has long been one of my least favorite celebrities, but he's becoming my hero for ranting against the cancel culture.

We have the moral high ground on this, and it's great when left-leaning liberals join us on the fundamental principles that free societies are about persuasion, not coercion. The so-called progressive left wants to bully people into doing what they perceive as righteous, and it's important to call them out for being bullies.

Brad Lips
But is there a best way to lean into this cultural challenge? John said it's important to call out the bullies. I sort of love that recent years have seen the rise of "snowflake" and "Karen" as slang that ridicules, to a certain extent, these overly timid or overly controlling mindsets. But I don't know if that's changed anything. Is there a more constructive way to engage and persuade people?

John Tillman
I am completely and fully on board with ridicule.

Jim Otteson
Well, Voltaire is alleged to have said that if you want to know who has power in society, it's whoever you're not allowed to laugh at.

Lenore Skenazy
Wow.

Jim Otteson
Yeah, which is pretty profound, but, Brad, you asked that question as if it's an either/or situation. I think it depends

on the context. Usually, with audiences that don't agree with us, it's important to begin with something that doesn't antagonize them, something that shows there's some kind of common ground. So here's a proposal: let's address identity politics by acknowledging that, yes, we have identities, and these identities are informed by our social and historical past. That's all true. But, also, we aren't reducible to those identities.

We are individuals with agency, and the most important factor in your life is you. You don't need to be happy with the cards you're handed in life, but you still have to play. You still have to live. And how we choose to live may be informed by our histories, but it is not determined by them.

This is one of the things that I love about the Let Grow philosophy, that each person deserves to step up to the responsibilities of life and experience the consequences of their actions.

Lenore Skenazy

And many, many kids are being deprived of this, which is why Let Grow tries to actually change behavior by recommending that schools give homework assignments along the lines of, "Go home and do something on your own that you are hesitant to do." This also pushes the parents to let them finally do something new.

Let me share some of the responses that came from a seventh grade class. This is what they are hesitant to do: "I was hesitant to try walking my dog alone because I was scared that he would get loose from the leash or a scary man would take me." "I was afraid to climb a tree because I was scared I was going to fall and break a bone." "I wanted to try doing a wheelie on my bike, but I was scared I would hurt myself." "I was afraid to try and cook because there's an open flame and I could get hurt." And, "I was hesitant to use a sharp knife as my parents had never let me before."

Brad Lips

Oh, that's depressing. And it makes sense that a twelve-year-old who asks mom to cut their food might become a twenty-two-year-old who can't handle being challenged with new ideas. I'd like to keep exploring the question of what is to be done to persuade communities that seem increasingly close-minded.

Lindsay Craig

A big part of what I'm doing at National Review Institute is reminding people that there was an era—and, of course, I use Bill Buckley as the great example—where people actually disagreed rather completely on an issue, but engaged in a respectful way.

You could have a civil discussion on an issue and really learn a lot more about it, taking lessons from both sides. You would also come to appreciate that the art of persuasion actually requires you to show respect to others. Respect and civil discourse is not what you get today on Twitter. It's about shutting someone down, and maybe doing it in a cooler way or faster way than others. Everything in the system now incentivizes *non-civil* discourse and not being thoughtful about opposing views.

It makes me really worried about our civic culture. And it's important to note that, while we often identify this new intolerance with the political Left especially since they have the cultural power to abuse it, there are also ugly tendencies of the political Right, and this has been going on for years, and the Trump phenomenon exacerbated it rather dramatically.

John Tillman

Could you expand on that—the conflict on the right—Lindsay? Who's conflicted with whom and over what?

Lindsay Craig

Mostly I'm referring to the Team Trump phenomenon of saying you're with us or you're against us. Critiquing the president in any way, shape, or form, is giving aid and comfort to the enemy, so you should be banished from the tribe. That's an unprincipled response, and while I get where it's coming from, it doesn't lead anywhere productive. You're legitimizing the same tribal thinking and bullying that the hard Left uses. So I'm just trying to say that, using air quotes here, "our side" has some real fractures to heal.

Brad Lips

When I'm asked by friends abroad for my take on the meaning of Trump and conservative populism, I begin by explaining how excited I was about the Tea Party movement of 2010 and 2011. This was a movement genuinely focused on limiting government and respecting the constitutional framework of the US, but the media coverage it received was incredibly disingenuous. The media invented accusations of racism with no basis other than the fact that Tea Partiers disagreed with President Obama's agenda.

After the Tea Party movement fizzled out, the victim of bad media and a politicized IRS, Trump was able to pick up the pieces. He was a guy that took punches from the media and punched back. They liked that, and as a consequence the conservative populists started defining themselves as "anti-elite," rather than staying attached to an abstract ideological project. Trump's agenda was a mixed bag—some policies that fit the ideological project, some policies that made us wince—but, to Lindsay's point, Trump's loyalists embraced it all and redefined the Republican Party in the process.

I continue to believe that most in this community are limited-government people at heart, but given the polarizing arrogance of much of the American media, that movement has been pushed into an anti-elite identity politics. Niels, is there any parallel to this in Canada?

Niels Veldhuis

I don't know of cross-country data on this topic, but we certainly don't seem to be as polarized in Canada as is the US, though the reasons why are complex.

For all Trump's faults, he certainly showed strong conviction to some of his beliefs; in Canada there's much frustration that conservative politicians often shy away from standing up for any real principles. To get elected they water down their ideas. I just don't think that's a successful approach either. So for the moment, our politics are not as heated, but I do always worry that what we're seeing now in the US might also make its way to Canada three to five years from now.

Brad Lips

I now see that our friend Avik Roy from FREOPP [Foundation for Research on Equal Opportunity] has joined us. Avik, you're just in time for me to turn the conversation to the policy questions we need to worry about. Where should classical liberals be putting their energy in the decade ahead?

Avik Roy

Well, I got into the public policy world because of concerns about deficit spending and where that leads our country, and the developments of the last year have heightened those concerns considerably. The Federal Reserve has expanded the monetary supply by 25 percent, effectively devaluing all the dollars that people hold by 20 percent, and there's no end in sight for the use of this policy device in the United States. Other countries have adopted this strategy too; monetizing debt allows the government to increase spending without the political challenge of raising taxes. But this form of stealth taxation power creates some dangerous policy outcomes.

We should be mindful that we're approaching the hundredth anniversary of the *denouement*, the Weimar hyperinflation. We've really opened this can of worms here in the US, and I just don't see where it ends because the populist approach to fiscal policy is to spend more money and not increase taxes. That's what people in a democracy generally want and that's what we've been doing. Germany actually is the only country that's really fought that tendency successfully, perhaps because of their experience with Weimar. And now, we have the added variable of technologies like Bitcoin, that allow for an escape from devalued Western currencies in a way that didn't exist before. Now, it's an extremely important milestone in economic freedom that people have an alternative to irresponsible fiscal and monetary policies by governments. But people who don't appreciate the danger of those policies, and remain in devalued currencies, will be left behind in a crisis.

Jim Otteson

I'm on board with you, Avik. Sometimes I frighten my students by talking to them about the debt and what their share of the debt is. And I say things like, "Well, the most recent $1.9 trillion package that was passed, that's going to mean $5,000. So maybe your family or you get a $1,400 check, but you're going $5,000 more into debt." "Wait, what? How does that work?"

But the problem is made even worse by the passive approach to life that we've commented on—this sense among millennials or younger that someone out there will solve their problems. You calculate the debt and the net present value of all these off-budget entitlement programs, and you present them with these astronomical numbers, they say, "Somebody will figure it out."

I try to explain that older generations are living well at the expense of their generation and future generations that don't even get to vote. It's a little like "taxation without representation," something we once fought a revolution over. But they tend to shrug it off. I would think being an adult would mean taking ownership of your own life, and taking stewardship of the institutions that have made America an exceptional free society. That's unfortunately lacking right now.

Avik Roy

The point you're making, Jim, that resonates with me a lot is the further you get away from these real crises of the past—the Great Depression, the Weimar era, World War II—people forget what a real civilizational collapse is like. Of course, throughout history, it is in those moments where people forget what civilizational collapse is like, that's when it happens again. I don't know what we can do about that.

John Tillman

The disbelief that it could happen here within this context is fascinating to me—especially given what is literally happening right now in our society with the de-platforming of certain views, with the consideration of creating "vaccine passports" that could be abused for social control like China's Social Credit System.

I had conversations with a left-leaning friend eighteen months ago and said, "Look at what's happening with the cancel culture. You're worried about the illiberalism and norms being flouted by Trump, but look at what your own team is doing." He dismissed it. He couldn't believe we'd see a tyranny of the mob here in America, but of course, it is literally happening.

Lindsay Craig

Another area where things have unwound pretty fast is in public safety, with the "defund the police" movements and so on. This again is where we see the danger of not learning your history.

One example is the city of Baltimore, which just decided to stop arresting people for petty crime. Of course, the policing revolution in the 1990s that made New York and other cities flourish was this exact idea—from James Q. Wilson and George L. Killing, popularized by Manhattan Institute—that enforcing petty crime [laws] can have a disproportionate effect in taming crime more broadly. That is just so fundamental to good policing and positive relationships with the community. For American cities to abandon this strategy, it's a disservice to the citizens who live there. We're in for a repeat of the 1970s: crime will spike and people with wealth will flee. Now that remote work options are commonplace, who knows if they come back.

Jim Otteson

And to Avik's point, here comes the federal government to issue debt to bail out jurisdictions that made irresponsible decisions, so they don't suffer the terrible consequences of those decisions. How many billions will Illinois get from this or the next bailout to solve its pension crisis? Future generations will pay the bill for today's mistakes; that's a losing moral proposition and it might help persuade some people who say they're inclined toward socialism.

Brad Lips

I see an interesting parallel here with the earlier part of our conversation. Lenore's work reveals how tough it is for kids to develop resilience if they have a helicopter parent hovering around to ensure they never get in a fight or never have their feelings hurt. Bailing out jurisdictions that made irresponsible decisions similarly creates a moral hazard and insulates decision-makers from the consequences of their bad policy.

Is the depressing lesson of this conversation that, just as we should make sure our kids get a chance to resolve their own problems, we actually need to experience the consequences of bad policy to recharge interest in classical liberal ideas that work?

Jim Otteson

I definitely don't like arriving at a conclusion along the lines of "They get what they deserve" because, really, the people who will tend to suffer within these dying cities are precisely the people that we should be most concerned about, those who have the least ability to move or to leave. Too much is at stake to be fatalistic about these issues.

Niels Veldhuis

You know, this question—do things have to get worse before they get better?—is really quite impossible to answer. What I think we need to do is look at history and consider that you can never tell what will be the little catalyst for massive positive change. This just means we've got to do everything we can to work for greater economic freedom; and the bigger presence our movement has, the better our chances of getting positive reforms before we come close to hitting the wall.

And we can never lose sight that some of the major figures that came before us—from F. A. Hayek to Milton Friedman— they were lonely and isolated for decades before their impact really emerged. So while we might be pessimistic in the short-term, we should realize that—especially in a world with greater mobility of capital and of people—there will be free societies to hold a light up for the world, and we shouldn't underestimate the extent to which our work can make a big difference in achieving a better future.

Jim Otteson

Yes, and I'd posit that, as organizations connected to Atlas Network work for policy reform, it's crucial that they emphasize this idea about individual agency. Free societies may never be perfectly fair societies in some abstract sense, but what is special is how they can offer legal equality and opportunity like no other.

John Tillman

What you just said, Jim, and what we've been talking about, is an absolute threat to those that practice this identity politics racket. It's why our message should be appealing. What we are saying to people is that you don't need the government to solve your problems. You don't need a central authority to solve your problems. You can solve your own problems. The path of aspiration is better than a path of dependency.

Chapter Seven
Avoiding a New Lost Decade
in Latin America

Can the next decade be one of progress in Latin America? What factors have made "neo-liberalism" a slur in Latin American countries that have embraced populist leaders? Where might we find a country that could set a positive example for the rest of the hemisphere in the years ahead? These are some of the important questions that emerged in this January 2021 discussion among thought leaders from Latin America.

All of our participants are collaborating now in the work of Atlas Network's Center for Latin America, which was launched in 2019. The Center is directed by *Roberto Salinas-León* of Mexico who also serves as president of the Alamos Alliance. *Antonella Marty* is an Argentine author of *Capitalism: The Antidote to Poverty* who regularly appears in Spanish-language media. *Gonzalo Schwarz* is a recently naturalized US citizen who emigrated from Uruguay and who founded the Archbridge Institute, a think tank focused on social mobility. *Juan José Daboub* is the former managing director of the World Bank and minister of finance of El Salvador.

Brad Lips

Let's start our conversation by looking forward ten years. When Atlas Network celebrates its fiftieth anniversary in 2031, what do we hope our movement will have accomplished in Latin America that might seem aspirational today?

Roberto Salinas-León

Our big goal needs to be a reversal of the rising tide of illiberalism that we see today nearly everywhere, and this requires being willing to innovate and rebrand the freedom movement so the principles of liberty are recognized as the principles of everyday citizens.

The opportunity we missed in the past was to cheer on smart economic reforms that took place in parts of the region in the 1980s and 1990s, without concerning ourselves with educating people broadly about why human dignity, free enterprise, well-defined property rights, and rule of law are all interconnected. After the ravages of devaluation and the encounters with authoritarianism that marked "the lost decade" in Latin America, leaders turned to our ideas because they were out of options. It became pragmatic to open borders, to stabilize the unit of account, and to privatize government monopolies. Sometimes these moves were done for the wrong reasons—to raise funds to cover a fiscal deficit, for example—and we did not succeed in explaining the *correct* reasons that everyone has a stake in liberal institutions.

It is perhaps understandable, after fighting communism and military dictatorships, that the liberal community of the last generation should have been content with the gains that were made, but if we are to reboot our cause and seize this idea of a freedom movement 2.0, we need to win the moral high ground and become a more relevant voice in public discourse so there can be a lasting consensus about why everyday citizens' interests are aligned with our principles.

Juan José Daboub

Perhaps to complement Roberto's important comments with a measurable goal, I would hope that a decade from now there will be at least eight Latin American countries that are investment grade, high-income countries, and that two of them will rank among the top five countries in the global *Index of Economic Freedom*. This will mean people in Latin America will have their destiny in their own hands, and the region will have excellent examples of how economic and social progress can be achieved.

Further, in ten years, I would hope that the community of organizations that rally around Atlas Network will be recognized for having reenergized the ideas that worked. It will be a wonderful contribution if, when we look at the countries that will have become success stories, we can say, "We helped the key reformers to refine their agenda, we added very specific communications tools, and we helped them gain enough political capital to be successful"—not once, but several times, so we know it is a replicable strategy.

Gonzalo Schwarz

Yes, if we could achieve Juan José's goal, I think the region would look very much changed: more prosperity, more opportunity, and more social mobility so that the inequality we see now in the region is not felt as pervasively or acutely.

Part of the problem is that we have had inadequate leaders, to say the least. The *caudillo* mentality is a mentality of power, so leaders don't focus on the long-term institutions that will help produce lasting economic growth. They are concerned with redistributing wealth to increase their personal power.

This is why the biggest challenge today, which will likely be the biggest challenge for the next ten years, will be to improve the rule of law. The lack of strong, formal and informal legal institutions and the prevalence of bureaucracy in the region feed into a kind of everyday corruption that keeps a lot of the economy in the informal sector and outside of networks of higher productivity and exchange. This in turn keeps most people feeling very much like they do not have opportunities for themselves and their families.

This also ties into a challenge about the narrative around freedom; even though in countries like Venezuela the lack of freedom is very palpable, for most people in the region the concept might sound like an abstraction that's very separate from what people actually think about when considering how their lives could be more successful and purposeful.

Look at what has happened in Chile. Because of more economic and individual freedom there was a lot of improvement in social mobility, with low unemployment, lower poverty and inequality levels, compared to other countries in the region. But it is human nature to want more, and as the improvement engine slowed down in Chile over the past decade, even as freedom continued to flourish, a backlash emerged at this sense that it is unjust that opportunities are still too scarce; the sense of more economic freedom wasn't enough.

Antonella Marty

The problem that is emerging in Chile is exactly what has long plagued my native Argentina. There was such hope around the election of Mauricio Macri in 2015, that maybe the specter of Peronism had been vanquished. But the structural reforms that are needed to take up the fight against corruption and create broad-based economic opportunity were not undertaken while he had the political capital to make changes.

So this old mentality has won the day again—the belief that a big state must ride to the rescue, when in fact, the big state is the source of many problems. With the COVID-19 situation, Peronist demagogues like President Alberto Fernández realized they can use the pandemic to promote even more populism and more state interventionism than would happen in regular times.

Perhaps that is the real ten-year goal: to understand the persistence of Peronism and other flavors of populism in our region and to counter it with ideas that are demonstrably better for all levels of society.

Brad Lips

Perhaps we should look at Juan José's experience in El Salvador as a case study for how a country can change in a positive direction but also hit unfortunate road blocks.

Juan José Daboub

Yes, remember that El Salvador is a country that went from hardship to investment grade in a relatively short period of time. El Salvador was the last true battle of the Cold War. During the 1980s, 5 percent of our population was killed and 22 percent of our population migrated, primarily to the United States.

But in a period of six years—from the peace agreement of 1992 to 1998—we emerged from that very dark picture into a country with investment-grade level debt. Not only that, in 2000 and 2001, *The Index of Economic Freedom*, published by The Heritage Foundation, and *The Wall Street Journal* ranked El Salvador as the thirteenth-freest economy in the world, ahead of Chile and Germany and many other countries.

So what worked? We had an alignment among political leaders, the private sector, and a society that was desperate to rebuild from the war. Thankfully, we adopted the right principles and values. We benefited from expert advice, so President Cristiani brought many of the Chicago Boys [economists who advised on economic reforms in Chile] to El Salvador. He wanted people who had been successful in the past. So we put into practice these ideas. We opened up the economy. We restructured and deregulated state-owned enterprises. We minimized regulation and maximized competition. We even closed the central bank and adopted the US dollar as our legal tender. All of that took El Salvador to a great position in terms of economic freedom. We were not yet Singapore, but we were certainly going in that direction.

So what happened? Well, it takes a generation—twenty-five or thirty years—for reforms to cement. But we eventually ran out of strong leadership to advance this goal. The presidents that followed were corrupted; one former president is in jail and another is in political asylum in Nicaragua, but worse than what they stole is that they stopped the process of reform, and El Salvador has in many ways gone backwards over the past dozen years. And the current government is following the same path towards decadency. Another lesson we might have learned earlier is that our near exclusive focus on economic reforms left a missing piece. A lot of progress took place—we cut poverty by half, life expectancy expanded by five to six years, we saw health improving by many metrics, but we didn't have enough resources and time to do as much in the social sectors as we did in the economic sectors, nor did we have a chance to further strengthen institutions, for example in the judicial system. As I said earlier, it takes one generation to make reforms and one generation to cement them; we were halfway through the reform process when we fell into the wrong leadership of the country.

Roberto Salinas-León

Juan José's long-term perspective here reminds me that we should not take for granted the progress that has been made.

Imagine if this conversation were held at Atlas Network's founding in 1981. If I told you things that indeed came true—that Mexico would become the US's number one trading partner, or that we would have monetary stability in Mexico, and Colombia, Peru, Brazil, and El Salvador, for that matter—it would have been more reasonable to predict a Martian invasion! Where we had military dictatorships, we have liberal democracies, fragile and fallible though they may be. This is progress.

To be sure, the tasks ahead are daunting. Reports on economic freedom and Institutional Quality tend to rank Latin American countries very low on rule of law, contract enforcement, judicial independence, and property rights with very low scores, and there is no cookie-cutter recipe to successfully plant these important institutions. I'm reminded of the quip of Gordon Brown about developing a reliable rule of law, "The first five hundred years are the toughest."

Latin American countries have wrestled with this challenge alongside terrible damage stemming from the war on drugs, launched by the US in the 1980s, and experienced in Colombia, Mexico, Peru, Bolivia, across Central America, and now Venezuela. Important parts of these countries became "failed regions" where peasants and families were literally enslaved to work for the likes of El Chapo, Pablo Escobar, or members of the FARC. The death toll and damage to potential prosperity from the drug war has been staggering.

Yet, against all odds, several of these countries were able to make the leap forward to become credible and internationally recognized democracies. When the election of Vicente Fox in Mexico ended seventy-one years of the PRI's "perfect dictatorship" in 2000, or when Patricio Aylwin was elected to replace Pinochet in Chile in 1990, there was a popular sentiment similar to the fall of the Berlin Wall, as political freedom and liberal democracy took these steps forward.

So, making strong progress on rule-of-law issues in a ten-year timeframe is a challenge we should embrace. In fact, "thinking big" in this way is almost certainly a necessary precondition for *achieving* big things.

Gonzalo Schwarz

One cause of optimism on the rule-of-law front is that the younger generations have less patience for corruption, and they can easily raise awareness of violations of the public trust with the communications tools we have available now. That's how some of the Arab Spring revolts happened, and you can see it in the protests that brought down President Dilma in Brazil in 2016 and that bolstered the courage of the Brazilian prosecutors who brought to light the Operation Car Wash scandal in that country.

We can be hopeful that social media tools will be used to keep pushing back against government corruption, and of course they can also help us convey to target audiences how these issues of a weak rule of law and pervasive political privileges are keeping regular people off the ladder where they could reach more opportunities.

Antonella Marty

It's worth mentioning here how countries seem to differ in the extent to which they resist truly outrageous abuses of political power, abuses that undermine the rule of law. I would posit that Venezuela is the most corrupt country in Latin America, with the possible exception of Cuba. Of course, we know very little about Cuba since it is a very closed society.

As worrisome as Argentina's populism is at this moment, there is still a belief in the country's constitution in a way that no longer exists in Venezuela. Cristina Kirchner could not have become a dictator had she tried, as Chavez became in Venezuela. At the end of 2020, President Fernández tried to expropriate a company in the rural province of Santa Fe, and the public outcry was tremendous. At some level, Argentines still know the importance of the rule of law, whereas Venezuela is very much lost to a narco-dictatorship ruled by a mafia that's allied with Hezbollah and Hamas and Marxists guerillas, with no genuine accountability to the people and the rule of law.

My point is that it's gotten to this terrible state because there was anthropological damage done in the Venezuelan society, whereas Argentines benefited from a very strong, classical liberal constitution, written in 1853 by Juan Bautista Alberdi, who was inspired by the US founders. Peronist governments tried to destroy that constitution, but we still have it. It is still a pillar to defend and promote democracy and liberty in Argentina.

Roberto Salinas-León

As an important footnote, let's credit Alex Chafuen during his long tenure as president of Atlas Network for reminding us—I remember him saying it back in the mid '80s—that we should look at our own cultural roots and intellectual traditions. Yes, of course, we admire the Friedmans, Hayek, and so on, but Alex said, "Look at your own history," and that was a great contribution. Indeed, I discovered Mexican liberals of the nineteenth century such as José María Luis Mora and Lucas Alamán, and fantastic classical liberal thinkers in Argentina and even Venezuela.

So I do have hope for Venezuela, because there's a tradition of liberty there too. Knowing that it can be found . . . that is something for which I'll be grateful to Atlas Network, and it is something that we should share with future generations.

Antonella Marty

Yes, and of course we have contemporary heroes that provide inspiration too. When I think of what Rocio Guijarro and the CEDICE team are doing in Venezuela, it is huge because they are really facing a dictatorship from the inside.

Brad Lips

While it is important to talk about those who inspire us in a positive way, we would probably be remiss if we talked about intellectual trends in Latin America without discussing the role of Pope Francis during these last seven or eight years of his papacy. The first Latin American pope—obviously with a sincere compassion for the poor—comes at the question of "what to do" with the same suspicions of free markets that we see among many of his fellow Argentines. Is it fair to say that Pope Francis (and his enormous culture power) has set back the cause of liberalism in the region?

Roberto Salinas-León

It is an important question. My short answer to that is yes. You might say Pope Francis demonstrates that the road to hell is paved with good intentions, because there's no question that he's genuine and that he's sincere and that he empathizes with the plight of those that continue to live in extreme poverty. But the fact remains that the leaps forward the poor have made over recent decades have been because of trade, because of the stability of the unit of account, and because of the entrepreneurial drive of so many Latin Americans who, despite red tape, find ways to get ahead.

Pope Francis's message has stressed the opposite. His message has resonated with those whose ideology is highly paternalistic, such as our own President López Obrador in Mexico. AMLO (as he is known) believes he has privileged access to moral truth, and therefore his opinion is the only legitimate basis for determining how wealth should be redistributed, and that anyone who questions his leadership is acting in bad faith. In large part I think that is a consequence of this unfortunate turn that Papa Francisco has taken.

Antonella Marty

Yes, I think Pope Francis's mentality *is* the mentality of Argentina in general. And today he blesses everything this Peronist government is doing in Argentina, and it seems that is because he shares this view that everything in politics is very binary. It is as though, if you are against President Fernandez in Argentina, you must be a fan of Donald Trump or Jair Bolsonaro.

I was speaking a few weeks ago with [economic historian] Deirdre McCloskey, and she remarked that those of us who identify as libertarians or classical liberals, we are nowhere in the left/right map, but that's the map that most people use to navigate conversations of politics and economics.

I would have to hope that objective observers will look at the disastrous course that Argentina has taken and realize there must be an alternative. Argentina, in the *Doing Business* report, ranks 126th among the countries of the world, right next to Paraguay and Iran. Argentina used to be one of the most important countries, but Peronism changed the trajectory seventy years ago, and the curse persists. It persists because political leaders can enrich themselves through Peronism, and we have failed to help the broad public understand the immorality of it all.

Brad Lips

One idea that I see emerging from this conversation is that our intellectual movement has a two-pronged challenge. On one hand, we must recognize that liberal reforms will require having political leaders with the determination to make structural reforms, and the strength to resist the temptations of corruption, especially given the new reality Gonzalo described. On the other hand, we need to improve how we offer our ideas, so they cohere into a narrative that people understand as an alternative to the populism and statism that is now on the march.

Juan José Daboub

I agree with Brad and so we have to do something about it. It would be great if one could emulate what worked for us in El Salvador, but add more effective political communications to create sustained success. I favor a model that I refer to as a Policy/Political Strategic Advisory and Working Team. To implement free-market reforms that have proven to bring about the inclusive prosperity we seek, a Working Team like this could operate as a "shadow cabinet" in the British tradition—that is, providing a sounding board of experienced reformers and credible policy experts that can work with a government of any persuasion on these goals.

We need to better deploy knowledge of past reforms and of new innovations in the field of policy ideas and help leaders who share our vision be strategic in how they build enough political capital for one particular reform and finish with even more political capital to do the next reform—thereby creating a positive snowball effect to improve institutions across society.

Gonzalo Schwarz

When it comes to the question about the narrative, I see that it's important to explain why Venezuela and Cuba have failed. But the bigger challenge is to "read the room" and understand the topics that people are thinking about in their day-to-day lives.

If they are angered by the inequality they see, let's start there and persuade them that the problem is best addressed by looking at whether people are blocked from climbing the income ladder. Let's appeal to the aspirations that normal people have with concrete solutions that bring opportunity and social mobility. My point is just that we must start by playing in the field where people already are. We can't expect to bring people to our side when we're outside of the field itself.

We need to give the benefit of the doubt to those who worry about inequality. A lot of people see poverty and they think, mistakenly, that the reason some people have less is because some people have more. Let's get into that conversation and say, "Yes, I worry about the poor as well, but the problem seems unlikely to be solved by punishing the wealthy. What I think you're looking for are ways to allow more social mobility."

Roberto Salinas-León

There are sophisticated intellectual arguments that Luigi Zingales and Raghuram Rajan have put together that can be guideposts for us in these next ten years. John Tomasi, too, because he also takes seriously the claims of social justice, but he redirects the focus where it really does matter for the disenfranchised.

None of this is reducible to an easy recipe. It's very hard work to translate that sophisticated philosophical line into a narrative that speaks to the day-to-day concerns of normal people. This is a great challenge we have, and it's something that we should embrace.

Brad Lips

Part of the great challenge, as I see it, is also to take ownership of the reasons why many Latin Americans conflate liberalism with cronyism, and why the "neoliberal" brand has such a stain on it. People see a conspiracy among elites in society and governments, so—while I agree that improving social mobility is a more logical goal than leveling inequality—I think we need to understand that the resentments so many feel are justified when the game is, in fact, rigged in many ways for those at the top.

And I honestly wonder what the answer is. It's one thing to tell business people not to act like cronies, but it's not so much a demand problem as a supply problem. The political favors are there. The supply will create its own demand. So I wonder: where can we look for an example of a country to learn from, where progress against cronyism has been made?

Gonzalo Schwarz

It is certainly difficult to think of a country that has resoundingly solved these problems, but obviously the United States provides a lesson to learn from. Perhaps this is less obvious today, as there has been backsliding in recent decades, but *The Prosperity Paradox* by Christensen, Ojomo, and Miller describes how the US had big problems with informality and corruption at the beginning of the twentieth century. Progress in the US came not so much from a specific change in the legal code, but because businesses got ever more dynamic and competitive, and people came to see that rewards through honest entrepreneurship were greater than through rent-seeking behavior.

Roberto Salinas-León

I'd answer the question by providing examples, not on a country basis, but by looking in certain localities. Look at the north and some states at the center of Mexico that have become highly immersed in global trade—Nuevo León, Baja California, Aguascalientes, Queretaro, or Coahuila—compared to Tabasco, Michoacán, or Chiapas in the south. There are two very different mentalities. So the improvement may not be apparent when you look at Mexico as a whole, but in parts of northern Mexico you get business done on the basis of competitiveness and real cost reduction, not political favors or lobbying for handouts from the federal government.

You might consider also Colombia. Fifteen years ago, everybody said, "I hope we don't Colombianize our society" with its endemic violence; but now it's, "I wish we could Colombianize our society!" How did they do it? A good part of that was Colombia's immersion in global trade, as there you have to respect the rule of the game. Whether you're a Maoist or a hardcore anarchist libertarian, global trade provides equality of opportunity, and you are incentivized to adopt norms of market liberalism. You can go country to country, and yes, there's corruption here and there, but I see progress in Brazil, in Uruguay certainly, in Panama, even Honduras and Guatemala.

Brad Lips
It is interesting that you highlight Colombia as it ranks highest among Latin American countries in the Global Index of Economic Mentality.

Gonzalo Schwarz
And Uruguay?

Brad Lips
That is one of the countries that lacks recent data, so it is not currently in our sample.

Juan José Daboub
Uruguay has, in my opinion, the conditions to lead the next wave of truly groundbreaking reforms, putting the individual at the heart of their public policies. Uruguay, today, has the leadership and the conditions to make this happen.

President Lacalle has assembled a cabinet of people working for the next generation and not for the next election. This is visionary. They understand the potential of implementing the "Uruguayan" version of what other nations have done to become freer, and they have the human capital of their citizens to implement it.

Gonzalo Schwarz
Well, as a Uruguayan, I certainly appreciate Juan José's comments that my home country can provide a blueprint for

success. It could be too early to tell what will happen, but the reason I'm optimistic about Uruguay is two-fold.

First, the change in the country has come from civil society. Voters saw how the fifteen-year rule of Frente Amplio's center-left coalition had submerged the country in economic stagnation and rising crime rates. Voices in the media and great think tanks like Centro de Estudios para el Desarrollo and Centro ESE, both Atlas Network partners, have highlighted these problems and suggested an alternative.

Second, we see leadership from the president and his cabinet, who have learned from and leaned on civil society organizations that want to break with the Caudillo mentality that is so pervasive in the region. It remains to be seen how things will turn out, but the early signs have been encouraging.

I'm hopeful that Uruguay's civil society leadership will stay active as a conduit between the public and a political leadership that wants to be an example for the region. This would be powerful to have a local example of success that others could emulate. After all, Uruguayans are no better than others in Latin America—except in fútbol, of course!—so we should be excited that other leaders may emerge in the region to enact the structural reforms we need.

After disastrous management of the pandemic and lockdowns from left- and right-leaning governments, people in the region are demanding better results from their leaders. It's an ideal time to be pushing to remove barriers that stand in the way of more prosperous and free societies.

Chapter Eight

Is This the Asian Century?

One of the great stories of the past forty years has been the escape from poverty of perhaps two billion people on this planet—the large majority of them Asian.

In 1981—the year that Atlas Network was founded—the World Bank calculated that 81 percent of East Asia lived in extreme poverty, as did 56 percent of the population of South Asia. Those percentages have seen incredible declines, to 4 percent and 13 percent, respectively, though the COVID crisis has surely caused a noteworthy uptick that is yet to be fully measured.

Will the countries of Asia be able to continue this economic progress? What will be the implications for Asians' political and personal freedoms? Those questions were at the heart of a conversation with longtime friends of Atlas Network held in February 2021.

Parth Shah is the founding president of Centre for Civil Society in India. *Chung Ho Kim* is retired from the Center for Free Enterprise in South Korea and is currently a visiting professor at Sogang University in Seoul. *Adinda Tenriangke Muchtar* is the executive director of The Indonesian Institute, Center for Public Policy Research and chief editor of Voice of Freedom Indonesia (Suara Kebebasan). *Simon Lee* is one of the co-founders of the Lion Rock Institute in Hong Kong.

Brad Lips

Let's begin by recognizing that the decline of poverty in Asia certainly ranks very high on the list of great things that have happened during our lifetimes. What do you see as the drivers of change in Asia over that period, and what is the unfinished business that exists for all of us who believe in liberty?

Chung Ho Kim

The case of South Korea might be instructive, as it enjoyed almost forty years of rapid economic growth after 1961 when President Park Chung-hee took power by coup d'etat. Classical liberals of course strongly dislike the human rights violations of his regime, but in the end Park sort of "imposed" more economic freedom and reduced the barriers to international trade; this, of course, allowed the Korean people to discover chances to make money. This was the driving force of the South Korean miracle, and its results are all around us.

What is unfinished business is solving the riddle: why don't people understand the principles that made possible their wealth creation? During my tenure with the Center for Free Enterprise, I saw my main goal was to persuade the Korean people that their miracle, their success, was created by the free market and globalization, and they should not take it for granted. But it seems right now that we failed. The free market and its defenders are considered an evil force right now in Korea.

Simon Lee

And may I interject one point about Korea? I watched the movie *Parasite*, which focuses on income and wealth disparities in Korea in a very critical way. Class resentments must be a big deal within the culture for someone to come up with a movie like that.

Chung Ho Kim

Yes, many people, especially the filmmakers and intellectuals, are convinced that South Korea is one of the most unequal societies in the world. Actually, if you look at the statistics measuring income inequality—you know, the GINI coefficient—South Korea is very much in the middle of the sample of countries of the world. It's the gap between reality and perception that made *Parasite* so popular. It reflects a mentality that sees free enterprise as basically immoral.

Brad Lips

Parth, you've been quite focused through the years on how economic freedom is understood in India, and you've been attentive to the filmmaking community in your country. Care to comment here?

Parth Shah

Yes, economic freedom has been a key focus. We came to realize in the early days of our institute, the Centre for Civil Society in New Delhi, that when we talked about economic freedom, people thought we were talking about the people with economic means, protecting the interests of the rich. The majority of Indians do not have any real *economic means*, so how could *economic freedom* matter to them? When we started to speak about "livelihood freedom," the same idea had a different connotation. It was seen as extremely relevant to anyone trying to earn a living. You don't think of the rich as trying to earn a living. Suddenly people realized our primary concern was for the people at the bottom, not the people at the top.

Once it was clear we were for the underdogs of society, we had a lot of Bollywood actors who were happy to participate in our Jeevika Film Festival (using the Hindi word for "livelihood"), and we were able to show terrific films on these themes. And of course, our policy work—on behalf of street vendors, micro enterprises, the budget private schools, the small farmers—also combined to convey this understanding that the market works for the bottom of the income pyramid as well as for the top.

Adinda Tenriangke Muchtar

On a similar note, in Indonesia we have made some significant progress despite a negative public perception of words like capitalism. We tend to talk about "economic empowerment" as we support efforts to streamline regulations for doing business, as right now it's maybe a hundred days to get a business license, and even then you may find overlapping local regulations that might still prevent you from opening for operation.

Removing these obstacles seems like common sense, but we are working against a strong anti-market mindset. I mean, we have a constitution that says clearly that the state is responsible for taking care of the people, so if you are seen promoting free markets and criticizing the government-run welfare state, it's quite a challenge.

But even here we are gratified to see progress. We translated Eamonn Butler's *An Introduction to Capitalism* and presented it in one of the big cities in North Sumatra—basically in a leftist base camp!—but we had really wonderful discussions with people who would come to understand, "Oh, this is what you call capitalism? We only know cronyism or state capitalism. Now I see it's not that." So, this educational effort is an important component of what we do both at the Voice of Freedom Indonesia and The Indonesian Institute.

Brad Lips

We began by talking about the miraculous drop in poverty that can be credited to an increasing embrace of markets across Asia. I was very taken with the history that Nin Wang wrote with Ronald Coase (just before Coase's death at age one hundred), *How China Became Capitalist*. That book showed how China prospered as a country when it loosened its grip and let bottom-up experiments blossom. The CCP didn't command China's marginal revolution from the top down, and yet I think that is the narrative being spread by the CCP and its apologists today.

Simon Lee

Yes, I think a different vision has hardened into place ever since people began talking about the "Beijing Consensus" in 2004. The idea was ambiguous at the time, but now there's a clear belief that the Chinese Communist Party wants people to believe a strong state apparatus can intersect with market economics and steer outcomes that have bigger political implications. Huawei, for instance, is a state-sponsored technology company. They want to not only grow domestically, but to achieve world dominance. And gradually, the people— not just the government—begin to believe this idea that the government can direct a more efficient kind of "capitalism" and that this is the way for developing countries to prosper.

We know that this kind of institutional arrangement sooner or later is likely to backfire, but it hasn't yet happened. Until it does, people will be likely continue to believe in the Chinese propaganda that their model is superior to the Pax Americana institutional arrangements—around free trade and such— that we have had in place since World War II.

Chung Ho Kim

Yes, and this fits with a mentality that I think is common for many Asian populations—I see it especially in Korea—this sense that freedom is given by the government, and that you are not born with these fundamental liberties to do what you want unless it is permitted by the government. The attitude matches very well with the COVID pandemic. People are well prepared to accept government direction.

Brad Lips
Interesting. Let's talk about how COVID-19 has played out, and possibly changed priorities, for different countries of Asia.

Adinda Tenriangke Muchtar
In Indonesia, we have seen this balancing act as the government tries to prioritize public health while understanding the economic reality that people are having trouble surviving with the economy shut down. It winds up being confusing, as we have new taxes so government can collect revenue, and then exemptions for small businesses, even subsidies for what they call "productive intention" but that has not been well defined and has been criticized by the public. We also have rampant cases of corruption regarding the social spending, involving even the minister of social affairs and the vendors of the in-kind social support.

Parth Shah
In India, our severe lockdown brought the economy almost to a stall. India probably is the worst performing economy in the world right now, with a more than 20 percent lowering of the GDP in the last five, six months of 2020. So there's a lot of pressure on the government to bring economic growth back, and the good side of this is that—with the focus on growth, rather than distribution—we see reforms that have been on a liberal wish list for decades.

An important one is agriculture reform, where we have had very restricted markets. The old monopolies that existed are getting broken down, so there's a huge reform in the Indian agricultural system that nobody was willing to even talk about seriously until now, and it is now getting done.

Secondly, instead of raising taxes to raise revenues, as in Indonesia, government has decided to privatize. So government is selling off its non-performing assets—selling off its stake in the nationalized banks, the insurance companies, as well as large tracks of land assets it holds in prime locations in many cities. This is now on the table, answering our long-standing call to privatize public sector companies.

The third positive thing that has happened is government's use of direct transfers instead of giving in-kind help. Instead of giving food or grains, which had huge leakages and corruption, the support is given as a direct transfer into the bank account of the citizen, which simplifies government's role and gives more autonomy to people receiving the benefit.

So, because we suffered very heavily economically, the government has defaulted to changes that seem in the right direction from a liberal point of view.

Chung Ho Kim

We haven't seen this reaction in Korea, as the number of COVID deaths per hundred thousand is very, very low for the East Asian countries. In South Korea, Japan, Taiwan, and Vietnam, the numbers are incomparably low compared to the Western countries. I wonder if it's because of this collectivist attitude, and the practice run we had with SARS eighteen years ago, that creates more obedience to the restrictions that are imposed and then some better health outcomes.

This is part of the character of many Asian countries, so if we are talking about this as an "Asian Century," we have to think about how, yes, Asian countries have provided growth to the world economy, but we are also introducing a governance model and atmosphere that enables totalitarianism again.

Brad Lips

Yes, it seems that economic freedom has brought a lot of prosperity in many parts of Asia, but there's also a deferential attitude toward authority that helps breed an arrogance within governments that are happy to take advantage of this to try to achieve political outcomes.

Over time, this has to erode the rule of law to a certain extent, and that's of course what has been so visible to anyone watching events in Hong Kong over the past couple of years.

Simon Lee

The drastic changes in Hong Kong certainly have woken people up to the real meaning of "the rule of law." Many people assumed that, if everything is written down and you have a judiciary and you have professional lawyers, that's the rule of law. But now we have a realization that the real question is: "If you take the government to the court, do you have a chance to win?" What we are realizing in Hong Kong is that what is written down beautifully in black and white does not matter, because decisions are made politically. And this means we do not really have the rule of law.

Once people realize that the checks and balances that should limit government have been corrupted, people no longer trust the government. There are all sorts of implications of such mistrust in Hong Kong. I would estimate more than half the people do not want to receive the COVID vaccine from the Hong Kong government because of this lack of trust. There are huge costs to running a society with no trust, and maybe especially for running an international financial center. For instance, if the government wants to borrow from the market, how much more would it cost if people lack the confidence that contracts will be honored?

On the contrary, we also see the government, for the sake of administrative expediency, does not go into the public tender. Some people who get contracts might have some relationship to the government, one way or the other. If you are close to the government, you know you won't have any negative consequences in case anything goes wrong.

This is the kind of corruption that ultimately collapses the institution.

Chung Ho Kim

I am reminded of how much Korea changed in the wake of the Candlelight Revolution that took place in 2017. That protest movement seemed to have good intentions, to stand up against corruption, but it has been like the French Revolution. Former president Park Geun-hye was impeached, and she is in jail right now, but this was achieved by really politicizing everything—even the judiciary and constitutional court. Today, if a judge makes a decision against the current president, then a Red Army type of activist community swoops in through Twitter or other social media. We used to have some kind of rule of law before the so-called revolution, but now it seems we have only rule *by* the law that is legislated by revolutionary congressmen to reward allies and marginalize rivals.

Brad Lips

Globally, this seems one of the worrying trends of our era. *The Economic Freedom of the World* report shows there's been some continuing improvement in economic freedom overall, but the rule of law indicator that they use has flat-lined or gone down.

So even though we find hope that Vietnam and other countries may be moving in a pro-market direction that would help a broad swath of the population enjoy greater living standards, we have to worry about the resilience of these societies, and whether prosperity can last, if rule-of-law norms fail to take hold.

Parth Shah

To fight the pandemic, governments around the world have acquired powers that are without any precedent. Much needed to be done to cope with the pandemic, but unfortunately this coincided with a larger populist wave that began well before the pandemic. That adds fuel to the fire, government intrusion goes beyond economics and into social and culture issues.

Part of the authoritarian tone of this moment shows up in how it's become more difficult to criticize government openly in the media. Old laws we inherited from the British colonial era, and never bothered to change, say you can be thrown into jail for "sedition," which is defined as saying almost anything against the government. These were not used in the past, so nobody thought about it, but it's increasingly routine to see government critics jailed on this basis. So this challenge concerning rule of law is linked to a challenge of free expression. Figuring out how to get powers back from the government, so we can enjoy the norms of a free society again, is a huge challenge for our movement.

Adinda Tenriangke Muchtar

This is actually a focus of a project that The Indonesian Institute is undertaking, with some support from Atlas Network, to highlight freedom of expression and the importance of data privacy. Nowadays, you need to worry if you claim, "My mobile has been hijacked," or something, as your only recourse is to give government authorities access to check whether this has happened, and of course it is reasonable to worry that, if you are seen as critical of the government, the authorities themselves might put something on your phone to track your activities or plant inflammatory content that could be used to discredit you.

There are cases where democracy activists, vocally critical against the government, have faced criminal charges. And there have been a number of polls—by National Commission of Human Rights, by Indikator Politik Indonesia, and by Indonesia Youth IGF, SAFEnet, and Pamflet Generasi—all showing strong concerns among Indonesians about freedom of expression.

So when our president, Joko Widodo, said in his current welcoming remarks of the launching of the 2020 Annual Report of the Ombudsman, "The public should be active in providing critical feedback regarding public service in Indonesia, including potential misconduct by the government," we respond, "Are you sure? Because the last time we did that, some of us were put in jail." You know, there is a reason The Economist Intelligence Unit has Indonesia declining in recent years in its scoring of democratic institutions, so that we rank behind Malaysia, the Philippines, and Timor-Leste. Reversing this trend and protecting free expression is therefore a big priority for both The Indonesian Institute and Suara Kebebasan.

Brad Lips

I'd like to get reactions to how the Chinese government's increasing totalitarianism and its actions are seen across the region, and if they have repercussions for how our liberal community can present an alternative to that model. Pew Research Center conducted a poll in the middle of last year, documenting how China is seen in an increasingly negative light around the world. As there's more evidence of duplicity in the early stages of COVID-19, human rights abuses with China's Uighur population, and the crackdowns in Hong Kong, can classical liberals use China as a foil to say, "We don't want a Beijing/CCP-style surveillance state here"?

Chung Ho Kim

When the Korean people have been surveyed about whether they would want to ally with China or the United States, as far as I remember it is about 80 percent that would prefer the US, and only 15 percent that choose China. But the current administration that is in power in Korea is very inclined toward

China. These are people who opposed the military regime in the 1980s and 1990s, so they claim to fight for democracy, but they are in truth very inclined to communism and socialism, and they see how the surveillance regime in China can be useful to advance their agenda.

Simon Lee

This returns us, I think, to some of the ideas from earlier in our conversation. Most people don't have an integrated view of what freedom is and what institutions support it. So they might oppose malevolent parts of the Chinese system, but they still feel alienated—to use a Marxist term—from "the free market," which they perceive as being about big transnational corporations. Our big task is to convey that economic freedom and political freedom can't be separated out. There is an overarching coherence to the liberal project.

After this pandemic, we have a tremendous opportunity to awaken people to what a mistake it is to depend on [governments], especially when they see for themselves how incapable governments have proven to be. The fight against the outbreak is indeed a very good example. For the threat to be over, everyone has to develop the resistance to the virus, whether through vaccination or acquiring the immunity naturally. You cannot depend on government slogans or them handing out money to make you safe. Those things can never make you safe. At the end of the day, it is your own immunity system that can save you from the virus.

So I get optimistic when I see people question government measures, whether it is mandatory masks or closing down the schools. People are beginning to see how absurd it is to impose one-size-fits-all solutions, mostly for the sake of administrative convenience and to be seen as "doing something," even if it doesn't seem to be working.

In Hong Kong especially, the pandemic is like a rerun of what we saw in 2003 with SARS. And a lot of people still have a vivid memory about SARS, when the government was not totally honest about the source of the pandemic coming from China, and at the very beginning government was so reluctant to disclose the details of the disease and things like that. In 2003, when the government refused to disclose the information about the virus, a group of citizen journalists started a website and started publishing the data, and that helped begin another movement of people who knew government could not be counted on to do the right thing. So perhaps the silver lining of COVID is that more of the world can see the behavior of the CCP dictatorship and other governments and realize people need to safeguard their interests as individuals.

Brad Lips
Let's close this conversation by backing up our perspective even further. Now that we are into the third decade of the 2000s, what are the odds that this will be remembered as The Asian Century, and will that be a good thing or bad thing for the well-being of humanity in general?

Adinda Tenriangke Muchtar
Well, I think it's a good thing that countries in Asia embrace this idea that our countries can flourish and bring more prosperity. The Japanese idea of the "flying geese paradigm" that was popularized in the 1960s gave the region a blueprint and a confidence it could grow, but it's important to understand that each country has to apply lessons within its own cultural context, and not just copy and paste what others do. What I hope is that an Asian Century can be built in the context of growth based on respecting individual freedom, where rule of law is secured and human rights are protected.

What would be dangerous is if—because countries like China or even Vietnam seem to be growing, despite not being democratic, and you might even argue they are better able to deal with the pandemic than can systems that balance the views of many democratic voices—people will be tempted to follow those models, so it's very important to rise up to this challenge to show that liberal ideas can effectively address problems of the pandemic and can revive our economies in its wake.

Chung Ho Kim

Yes, my comment is that, while this Asian Century may be good for the material well-being of Asian people and of all humankind, in politics it may represent a new illiberal mainstream—a mainstream that is collectivist and even totalitarian, that is led by China's Communist Party, and yes, the current regime in South Korea follows China in many respects.

Parth Shah

My hope is that we have an Asian Century that liberates almost everyone from poverty in Asia. That would be a very positive thing if that's what happens in the century and it is remembered as the Asian Century as a result. Perhaps another important dimension here could be a focus on mindfulness, or a spiritual dimension to life, which some Asian cultures prioritize. More of a balancing of material life and a broadly defined spiritual life—that could also be a very meaningful part of what could happen in the Asian Century.

The downside, as others have pointed out during this conversation, is a more authoritarian model of governance that has taken root in Asia. Singapore showed how to be a successful economy, and China has added even more to this idea of combining aspects of private enterprise with an authoritarian political regime. This is a bad lesson of the Asian Century, so we all should be dedicated to showing that achieving real prosperity and building a good society requires appreciation of personal as well as political liberties, just as much as economic freedom. Good societies need all the freedoms, not just one among them.

Simon Lee
Way before the 1997 Asian financial crisis, the World Bank talked about the Asian miracle. So many people in academia and government were so happy to have this example, which was in doubt after the end of the Soviet Union, that governments could indeed play a role in proactively promoting growth while maintaining their own institutional arrangements. The crisis of 1997 kind of wiped this out in a good way, and countries like Korea and Indonesia had to change because of this shock to the system and create more liberty for people to find new opportunities.

I don't know if we are anywhere close to catching this opportunity in the post-pandemic era, but I do think there's reason for hope. After all, an individual is the most basic unit in the economy, and the more they are able cooperate and compete, the better. Technology that connects us for a conversation like this, and allows us to work remotely, opens up a lot of opportunities. At the end of the day, national barriers will become less meaningful, and we will see more patterns allowing for people to work together. I think it is fantastic and a reason for hope.

Chapter Nine

A Wider Overton Window for
the Sick Men of Europe

The phrase "Sick Man of Europe" was first applied to the Ottoman Empire in the nineteenth century, but in 2021 it may need to be recast in the plural as almost every nation reels from the consequences of COVID-19 and its accompanying lockdowns.

But might there be a silver lining for champions of liberal reform? In February 2021, I convened a discussion of policy challenges and opportunities in Europe with experienced classical liberal leaders. We discovered a consensus that the Overton Window—the range of policy ideas that appear politically acceptable at a given time—has widened, both for good and for ill, in the aftermath of the pandemic.

Our participants included *Roxana Nicula*, the president of Spain's Fundación para el Avance de la Libertad; *Mark Littlewood*, general director of the Institute of Economic Affairs in London; *Clemens Schneider*, director of Prometheus Institute in Germany; *Alexander Skouras*, president of KEFiM (Centre for Liberal Studies) in Greece; and *Karin Svanborg Sjövall*, former president of Timbro in Sweden.

Brad Lips

Matt Ridley's new book, *How Innovation Works*, worries that Europe especially is strangling the dynamism that its economies desperately need because of its strong embrace of the precautionary principle. Where might we find bright spots that can help guide Europe forward toward innovation and much greater prosperity?

Roxana Nicula

Well, let's begin by confirming that it is a serious problem that governments of both left and right are bottle-necking every industry with regulation and reactionary ideas. Just last week, Spain's vice president, Pablo Iglesias, suggested creating a government-run alternative to Amazon, as though citizens need to be protected from the conveniences brought by a big American company. Our politicians wish Europe created its own dynamic companies, but they refuse to diminish the regulations that are a source of their power. It has been calculated that Spain's regional governments and the national one combine to produce over one million pages of new rules every year. How do new businesses survive, much less thrive, in a climate like this? Yes, we can find some bright spots in how Estonia is using blockchain processes to replace bureaucracy in some contexts, and in the pro-growth tax policies in some Eastern European countries, but broadly speaking, Europe handicaps itself in regard to innovation.

Mark Littlewood

Well, let me be the one to cheer you all up: it's all going to be fine! Post-Brexit Britain's going to save you all, so you can all relax and breathe out.

Okay, I'm not quite *that* optimistic, but since it's clear that the European Union doesn't have the capacity to reform itself from within, I do think we should be excited about how it might be reformed from without.

While the British government will quite certainly make a number of catastrophically stupid decisions in the weeks and months and years to come, the good news is that we now have some form of regulatory competition. In the case of the COVID vaccines, the UK government decided to cut through the red tape, take a gamble, license it quickly, and pre-order not knowing whether it would work; the European Union didn't.

That's one instance where the UK appears to have gotten it right and the EU got it wrong. If there are more instances of that moving forward, if indeed Britain is seen to roar ahead in certain sectors where it takes a more permissive course of action, then I lean optimistic that the EU will need to respond to this external pressure.

Alexander Skouras

Last week I was part of a Clubhouse event, discussing the chaotic rollout of the vaccine in Europe, and I asked a member of the European Parliament if there were any discussions taking place about how the EU can identify problem areas and make serious efforts to fix them. She responded by talking about an initiative by the European Commission to bring together partisan youth from around Europe, to craft ideas within their parties, and then get together to prescribe a new vision for Europe—a typical European solution that will not produce any kind of meaningful result!

So that's the negative side of Europe, but let's not over-generalize as though the EU is monolithic. We should give credit where it's due as it was a German firm (founded by two people of Turkish origin by the way) that developed the science behind the Pfizer vaccine—they're very credibly the heroes of the day. So yes, the EU is a slow and bureaucratic medium, but it only amounts to 1.5 percent of European GDP, and for that price at least it guarantees the free movement of goods, services, and people.

Clemens Schneider

Returning to this question of why Europe is failing to innovate, while I really love blaming the government for things, in this case I believe we must think about the mentality of European populations. Innovation is often conceived as a threat that is sort of dangerous or overwhelming. We all learned from the story of [Atlas Network founder] Antony Fisher that you have to change mentality before you change politics, so we can't expect the government to stop the supply of overregulation until we've done something to decrease the demand for it.

At this moment, the vaccine catastrophe is providing a window of opportunity where some are realizing, okay, the European Union cannot actually be depended on to take care of everything. We have a chance to have a big impact by reminding people that the soul of the European Union is simple and straight-forward: enabling cooperation through open markets. Of course, on the other side, we see efforts to enlarge the EU project well beyond its original purpose; for example, the German minister of finance was recently speculating about a common debt of the whole EU. So this is a moment when the liberty movement must be especially active because the debate could move sharply in either direction.

Karin Svanborg Sjövall

Yes, the jury is still very much out whether this is a fantastic opportunity or whether we just lost this one too. If I just look to our domestic debate in Sweden, the vaccine issue has launched a conversation I find quite heartening about the European Commission being way too centralistic. This is a kind of conversation that we haven't had in a long time. It's not going to change everything in a minute, but I think it's the precondition for things to be able to change.

But honestly, I'm fairly gloomy. I really am. One of the consequences of this pandemic is radicalization of both ends of our politics. I've been quite critical of the radical Right for some time, but now middle-ground parties are veering to the left in an extreme way.

The situation is not helped at all by having many companies shouting that they need more government support. So there really are a lot of problems piling up.

On the plus side, COVID has reminded us that the EU is not a health union, so we see many differences in how the pandemic has been managed and how the vaccine has been rolled out, and this is because we really do have different systems. And that makes it possible also to make interesting and important comparisons between different countries and their policies.

Brad Lips

Are there other areas where COVID has changed the conversation and allowed us to bring up topics that weren't in the public conversation previously?

Alexander Skouras

Let me offer some insights from what has happened in Greece, which elected a pro-reform government in 2019. During COVID, they really accelerated some very important reforms—not in a perfect way by any means—but they were reforms that we've been waiting for decades to see happen. This included a transition to digitized public services, which has happened with amazing speed and has replaced the worst kind of bureaucratic services. The move to e-government means less waste in the economy, but also less corruption because corruption breeds when there are lots of touch points where citizens interact with bureaucrats who have the leverage to negotiate favors.

So that's one very important outcome. And the other thing is that during a very severe economic crisis, there is a reflex to actually talk about what really matters. In the case of Greece, we had a year and a half of economic rebound after a ten-year crisis, and suddenly we're in a new recession with a nearly 10 percent decline in GDP.

The question becomes evident to policymakers, and it becomes even more evident to the public. The question here is growth. In normal times, the Left would say, "We want equitable growth." The Greens would say, "We want sustainable growth." Now everyone is hurting. They want their standard of living back. This is our opportunity because economic freedom is the surest way to ensure economic growth. And, of course, the fact is that growth via market reforms lifts our whole society and is both equitable and sustainable.

Mark Littlewood

To Alexander's point, the pandemic had many of us on our heels at the outset, but the opportunities to advance the classical liberal agenda are coming at us fast.

The Overton Window is now a much bigger window, right? You can hypothesize Europe going down an absolutely ghastly path, but I'm mildly optimistic over the next few years that the government will be pleading for any ideas that can stimulate economic growth.

When economic growth is ticking along at 2 percent, politicians can't be stirred to do anything controversial in order to bump it to 3 percent. But economies have gone backwards, so getting growth back into the economy is the absolute priority as soon as the sort of public health side of this subsides. And I think that in the UK, the government will understand they should reach for free-market levers to create that growth.

Karin Svanborg Sjövall

Even an awful pandemic can have a little silver lining or two. One that I've seen is that it's been awful for Green alarmists whose solutions have always been unworkable. The crowd around Gretta Thornberg has been asking us to stop flying and stop shopping. Well, we did all this now. I don't think anyone has enjoyed it, and the emissions still didn't go down enough to meet their targets, so I think we've now tried their experiment and can report that it didn't work. Surely they are not going away and will find new arguments, but 2020 provided real ammunition against their boldest plans.

Another disruption with an interesting outcome is that we've overcome enormous skepticism about digital healthcare providers. Now, hundreds of thousands of Swedes have gotten used to using them, and we're not going back. There are other economic sectors that similarly went through rapid changes to more productive models that wouldn't have happened in normal times.

But now, the gloomy bit. I think the worst is still to come in terms of political extremism, and that's because we have dire times ahead of us economically. What I learned in my work with Timbro's *Index of Authoritarian Populism* is that extremism spikes when there are external shocks. I would be very surprised if Europe manages to avoid it this time around. The contentious immigration debate of the past several years has receded while borders have been shut, but it will come back in full storm as people from poorer parts of the world again seek opportunity in Europe. That they will not be vaccinated to the same extent will add a layer of toxicity to the debate that we haven't seen before.

If unemployment goes up, we could see extreme turns on both sides. I wouldn't be entirely surprised if one or more European countries are subjected to more or less fascist government within two years, which would be the first ones since Portugal, Greece, and Spain all moved from dictatorship to democracy in the 1970s. Not all of Europe is moving this way, but there are definitely some tendencies that I find deeply worrisome.

Clemens Schneider

Yes, I certainly worry about the political extremes, and I have a feeling that radical ecological activists too will not be chastened by the lockdowns, but will rather argue that if we locked down the world for a disease with a mortality rate of 0.3 percent or whatever, we should do that much more given the predicted number of victims of climate change.

One question I want to raise is how we as classical liberals can counter these different illiberal groups. It's one thing to identify the fascists and the socialists and to present ourselves as not that. But I worry that by defining ourselves by what we are not, we fail to project an inspiring and likable explanation of what we are.

Brad Lips

What do you see standing in the way of that?

Clemens Schneider

Well, on one hand I see missing positive attitudes. Our reflex is to be grumpy about what others are proposing on inequality or racial injustices, but we shy away from actually involving ourselves in addressing those questions. That should change. I mean it's beautifully written in Hayek's *The Intellectuals and Socialism*; liberalism had become something of an administrative ideology by the 1930s and 1940s. Hayek saw that it needed to be recast as hopeful and Utopian, as something that people can really embrace.

Brad Lips

This may be a good time to turn to Alexander for insight about where liberalism is catching on, within your own country, Greece, and what is happening in parts of Eastern Europe. One of the notable findings of the Global Index of

Economic Mentality is that, when you're looking only at data from respondents under the age of forty, Eastern European countries lead the world in terms of their enthusiasm for economic freedom. Greece isn't among these high flyers on the GIEM, but I know you've seen a glimpse of a new dawn for our ideas there too.

Alexander Skouras

Well, you'll recall, Brad, that I moved from the United States back to my native Greece for precisely this reason in 2017. Surveys were showing liberalism as the most popular ideology among young Greeks as we moved into what I would call the post-populism era.

We had endured a coalition government of radical left and far-right parties for three years. We had self-proclaimed Golden Dawn Nazis elected to parliament. In the wake of that, young people began to reject left-wing and right-wing statism and violence. The pendulum has swung back against collectivism so that liberalism is now the most popular ideology, with 32 percent of the country identifying with liberalism, per a new poll that KEFiM (Centre for Liberal Studies) commissioned. That means that we, as the liberal think tank here, have an open door to advance a popular and authentic liberal agenda.

We, of course, have a very detailed libertarian policy agenda here to that end, but the other thing I want to note is that we should take it as our mandate to save the soul of liberal democracy. That's the real battle I see in front of us with alternative models getting popularity from dictatorial governments in China and Russia, and within the EU in Hungary and Poland. And for me, even as we build this big tent of liberalism in Greece, the goal we're looking for is not necessarily libertarian consensus, but to rebuild the consensus on liberal democracy first.

Mark Littlewood

Well, I'm a bit Churchillian about liberal democracy, the worst system in the history of humanity apart from all the rest. And I do think we can be ambitious here about the opportunity to make very big structural points.

We just released a paper to call attention to the failures of National Health Service saying on the face of the evidence so far, the National Health Service is nothing special. I mean, you would've thought we had called the queen a floozy for the reaction that we got; the deputy leader of the Labor party has gone absolutely bananas about it. But the fact is, we have triggered an opening where very serious newspapers are saying, "Haven't they got a point?" A year ago, such a report would have been rejected out of hand, asking, "Why are you against healthcare?" just as the IEA's calls in the 1960s to privatize the British car industry were met with, "Why are you so anti-car?" But now there's an opportunity in the wake of the pandemic to challenge the institutional structure in a way that was quite impossible previously.

I might say also that all the nanny state activities that our public health bodies had been doing now look quite like a distraction that took their eye off their main job. "You can't have cheap discounts on alcohol," or "You can't advertise bacon on children's television"—unless they're protecting us from bat soup imports from China, I don't think anyone thinks these should be our policy priorities anymore. You have one job, public health officials. It's pandemics. So, please, make sure I get the vaccine, and don't worry about whether I'm eating too many Big Macs.

Roxana Nicula

I want to add to Mark's comment about how the pandemic put health reforms on the table that would have been impossible earlier. In Spain, the government first tried to nationalize the private part of our healthcare, which only would have increased the dysfunction of our system, but in the end the policy solutions were liberal in nature. Doctors from other countries traditionally find it very difficult to get licensed to practice in Spain, but in 2020 our country granted licenses to almost 1,500 immigrant doctors, versus about thirty in prior years. That showed that, if there's a will, there's a way.

Another interesting cultural change accompanies the changes we see in remote working. Young entrepreneurs are learning they can flee the tax jurisdiction of Spain. YouTubers and other online content creators are moving to Andorra and setting this example that you can keep your money and avoid the obsolete bureaucracy that slows down progress in Spain.

Clemens Schneider

I'd like to go back to the concern about liberal democracy and suggest we need to be discerning about threats to this tradition in the UK, which are very low, and the threats in other parts of Europe—Poland and Hungary and some of their neighbors—which have moved in a worrisome direction.

It makes me think about my native Germany, which will see a transition to a new head of state this year after sixteen years of Angela Merkel, and the problem we have in standing up for values which should be important to us. I mean, I really admire how the current government in the United Kingdom is taking a very decisive stance on questions of human rights in this regard towards the governments in Russia and in China.

Governments such as those of Hungary and Poland have gone the other way and have allied with the world's illiberal powers, and I must say that Germany has been somewhat insincere in always trying to navigate a middle way. If the goal is to stay out of any conflict, you're bound to cave in debates like the one we've had about the Nord Stream pipeline from Russia.

So I really think classical liberals in Europe should do some real soul searching about how it's important to stand with protesters in Russia, Hong Kong, and Myanmar, and so on. Yes, it's important to rein in the welfare state, but let's not lose track of systemic questions about human rights.

Brad Lips

I very much like this theme of the importance of solidarity among liberals across the globe. I want also to turn the conversation to where there are other disruptive events on the horizon in Europe. Karin mentioned the migration crisis that fueled populist anxieties over the past decade; it's bound to return after the pandemic, and I wonder about the likelihood of another debt crisis as well.

Roxana Nicula

Quickly on the debt crisis question, of course, we have money that is untrustworthy so more monetary problems are inevitable. But also I prefer to look on the bright side of things: the increasing viability of Bitcoin, for instance, and what we might learn from those governments in Europe that have proven responsible in keeping debt below 30 percent of GDP like Estonia, Czech Republic, Bulgaria, Sweden, and Romania.

Karin Svanborg Sjövall

Well, I'll sound the gloomy note on this topic of sovereign debt. Yes, Sweden's national debt was 22 percent of GDP last year, a record low. But now it will rise to 31 percent, and we seem to be unlearning some very important lessons. We're told we need to spend more or there will be horrible populism everywhere. I seriously can't think of a better way to fuel populism than creating a system in which Germany and Sweden and other countries are paying in more than they feel they're getting back. We have had these tensions between north and south for a long time in Europe, and if they are stretched to a new breaking point, it really could be an existential issue for the European Union.

Mark Littlewood

I think that things are less predictable than ever, Brad. I just genuinely don't know whether there'll be a debt crisis. There could be, and you're right that we shouldn't wave it away, but I think the real take-away is that we just can't predict with any reliability what issues are going to be top of mind in two to three years' time.

For that reason, just as we talked about European economies needing resilience to see their way through a crisis, I'd suggest the same applies to our movement. We're going to have to show a real fleetness of foot. We're going to have to build a flexibility and dexterity into the movement so we can collaborate better, so we draw on one another's strengths, and so we can rise up to meet new topics when they become paramount in the public debate.

Alexander Skouras

I second what Mark said, and I'm going to point out that the pandemic stands out for offering an important lesson. As a movement, we weren't as prepared as we should have been. Some of the debates that came from the pandemic were just not on our radar screen, so the Overton Window, regarding how to deal with pandemic, moved completely towards the direction of big government.

We can't anticipate all the new challenges that will appear on the horizon, but the next pandemic might not be far away, so why don't we take stock of what we've learned over the past years and come up with a plan to deal with a pandemic that is more respectful of civil liberties, more respectful of economic freedom? This is the big challenge for now, and rising up to it will be a strong sign that, in contrast to bodies like the EU, we are open to learn from both successes and failures.

Clemens Schneider

Yes, thank you for that, Alex. I'm not sure I completely agree with you that our movement had little to say about most of the big issues that arose through the pandemic. But you drive home Mark's point that we need to be alert, we get our values right again, and we need to increase our connectedness to all the newspaper editors and professors who will play a role in creating conventional wisdom about how to respond to the next catastrophe. For me, this is a crucial point. We need to seek allies where we don't tend to seek or find them. Try to get in a dialogue with those who are a little far removed from us, so they at least have encountered our values.

Be better than the YouTubers that gain audiences by having one idea and disparaging everyone who disagrees. Be better so we have civil dialogue with as many people as possible. This is a very important job for us as liberals for the next decades.

Roxana Nicula

Yes, I quite agree that we need to be able to convey our values to all the stakeholders. Our foundation is quite happy that, after long efforts with unlikely allies, we are seeing some breakthroughs with even socialist tax directors in some Spanish cities. They have praised the usefulness of our research and undertaken some sensible reforms as a result.

I feel that Alexander's point is slightly unfair, in that I know our foundation was one of many that pivoted pretty quickly to take advantage of the COVID-19 Partner Response Fund that Atlas announced in April of last year, close to the beginning of the pandemic. Since then, through our ongoing campaign, Private Health Care Saves Lives, we've contributed to prevent even more damaging public policies from taking place in our country, like the government intent to apply 21 percent of VAT on the healthcare insurance policies for eleven million users. But, of course, we should consider how we could have been faster and how we might have gone on offense on this issue and others.

I mean, could there be a window of opportunity to think about the future of the European Union as concerns issues such as the free movement of people and capital, or reducing bureaucracy?

Maybe we could do something at the Atlas Network level that would give us the opportunity to start working on a major project for countries in the European Union with the goal of helping the European Union inspire more in the European Free Trade Association [EFTA model, a structure without hyper-bureaucracy integrated by Austria, Denmark, United Kingdom, Norway, Portugal, Sweden, and Switzerland]. In that way, Europe would have a chance to return to the path of its classical liberal origins.

Mark Littlewood

I do think we should explore how to work more effectively across the network on big topics. Even pandemics and disasters should be seen as learning opportunities, and there are going to be very important, comparative data sets that show how different countries and different systems have handled this pandemic. I mean the German healthcare system was excellent at the outset at distributing protective equipment, while the UK system was appalling. But the UK redeemed itself by reducing obstacles to getting out the vaccine. It's essential for us to be in this debate and to approach it honestly to discover evidence of what worked and what didn't. I suspect we'll learn that free-market liberalism will be shown to have been successful, and overregulated states less so. But we really need to pull those data sets together as they become available.

It is abundantly clear that we have a big role to play as we come out of this crisis, as we adapt to the lessons learned, and focus on the need for economic growth to supercharge the economy, which is becoming the top priority of pretty much every government on earth.

Brad Lips

Certainly, it seems more important than ever to liberate innovators and entrepreneurs to answer this need for growth.

If we can succeed in this, while also embracing Clemens's points about standing up boldly and unflinchingly for human rights, members of the broader public might finally get an accurate picture of the optimism, dynamism, and inclusivity that's at the heart of our liberal vision.

Chapter Ten
Africa at the Dawn of Its Continental
Free Trade Area

Africa failed to develop economically at the rate of other continents during the second half of the twentieth century, despite—or perhaps, because of—the generous flow of foreign aid from rich nations to impoverished ones. It seems increasingly clear that the primary consequences of those transfers were the propping up of governments unaccountable to their citizens and the undermining of local enterprise.

Should we be hopeful about Africa's trajectory in the twenty-first century? Internet access and mobile telephony have opened windows on the world to millions of young Africans searching for better lives for themselves, their families, and their communities. "Trade, not aid," goes the refrain, and the newly created African Continental Free Trade Area is establishing the largest free-trade zone in the world.

In February 2021, I convened a conversation about trends in Africa with four renowned experts. *Franklin Cudjoe* is the founding president of IMANI, a think tank based in Accra, Ghana; *Linda Kavuka* is based in Nairobi, Kenya, and is the director of African Programs at Students for Liberty and an advocate of the High Court of Kenya; *Ibrahim Anoba*, a Yoruba native of Africa pursuing graduate studies in the United States, is the managing editor of AfricaLiberty.org; *Magatte Wade* is a Senegalese entrepreneur and CEO of SkinIsSkin.com, who also serves as director of Atlas Network's Center for African Prosperity.

Brad Lips

The last time we held our Africa Liberty Forum in person, Dr. Martin Kimani talked about the task of "unleashing African genius" so that Africans can succeed inside Africa. He did that in the context of pointing out a tremendous demographic bulge: it is projected that 25 percent of the world's population will be African by 2050. A lot is at stake in whether the rising generation of Africans embrace rules of the game that are conducive to exchange, contracts, and the fundamentals of a commercial society. How optimistic are you from within your countries?

Franklin Cudjoe

Just before joining this conversation, I was watching a press conference with the minister for employment here in Ghana, and he was trying to dodge questions about his claim that three million or so jobs had been created in the last four years. He couldn't provide details on what kinds of jobs were created, and as youth unemployment stares us in the face, up and down and across the continent, the critical questions we need to ask are, "Where do jobs come from?" and "Where does economic growth come from?"

If the coming population surge manifests itself as projected, it can be an advantage as long as our economies are dynamic and growing, especially if the young people are bringing skills that will be needed in the economy of the future. So another side of this is whether education can be improved, so that Africa's human capital is ready to help us leapfrog to new technologies and other drivers of positive change.

Ibrahim Anoba

What Franklin just said is really important. How we are able to invest in education will really determine if this changing demography will be beneficial to Africa. It's an avenue where civil society can be helpful.

Of course, at the same time, we need to be breaking down the big problems like mass unemployment into smaller fixable problems, like getting more people into the formal economy and making it easier to start an enterprise. Fix these little problems first and you find it begins to have an effect on the big one.

So you need to have those changes that can liberate the poor parts of our societies, and the benefits in this case do not trickle down but rather trickle up. Trickle-up economics means that you start with the humble and the poor, securing the rights and the standing in law and the freedom to innovate that have been denied to them. That's what is needed.

The World Bank and IMF attach to their population projections some expectations about the growth of Africa's middle class. It's true that the consumer market of Africa should surpass that of China by 2050 in raw numbers. And, yes, it would be great if 115 million more Africans reached the middle class within three decades, but that part of their projection is a silly one in my estimation because it presupposes so much hard work to make enterprise easier and more open to everyone and not just the cronies at the top. African countries have many problems to overcome before they will generate the middle classes that the World Bank projects.

Brad Lips
Magatte, as an entrepreneur with operations in your native Senegal, you've compared doing business in Africa to swimming through molasses. Do you see changes happening?

Magatte Wade
Well, I always talk about poverty as the natural state of things when you have no wealth. Jobs are about creating

value, and to have value-creating jobs you need economic freedom. That's not just theory; it's the reality I have seen. I'm a big fan of the [World Bank's] *Doing Business* report, which provides a roadmap for how to improve the business environment for a country to do the reforms Ibrahim mentions. It does seem more countries are paying attention to their standing in the *Doing Business* report, but in typical fashion the governments try to game the system, just like they rig the game with democracy in much of Africa. So I worry that sometimes governments focus on how to improve a score in this report, rather than how to implement the authentic changes that would merit a better score.

So we need to pay attention to the real reforms and the real practices on the ground and not only to the issuance of this memo or that on reducing bureaucracy. Our job in civil society is to insist on real changes toward greater economic freedom. Fortunately, some countries are moving in the right direction. I'm so impressed for example with what Franklin and his team are doing in Ghana, but let's also be careful that governments follow through with real changes and not just more memos.

I agree that education is another part. I'm involved in several educational projects, and I am more and more convinced that education needs to be delivered by private actors. What I'm seeing in Senegal is that they say, "Let's put tech skills into the curriculum"—great, seems smart— "So you need to teach X, Y, and Z," and they're all old tech skills that haven't caught up with where innovation is happening. So I argue, yes, focus on education, but rely on the private sector to determine the content that will prepare young people for the future. Government ministries are never as forward thinking as for-profit entrepreneurs, and that's as true in education as it is in the tech sector or manufacturing or what have you.

Linda Kavuka

I'd like to take the conversation into another direction. Brad, you asked the question whether the rising generation of young Africans is embracing better "rules of the game." Thanks to the digital age, young Africans are much better informed and connected than in the past. They are willing to be more courageous, willing to stand up against corruption. You saw this in our neighbor, Uganda, recently as they cut off the internet because it was how people communicated to organize protests against the stealing of votes in the election.

So we can be hopeful that the younger generation, connected through digital means, could help us focus on better leadership. It will be difficult, because we are dealing with massive corruption, everywhere in the continent really. Ultimately, that election in Uganda was stolen because the government fought back with such violence that the people had no choice but to cave in. Back in October of last year, there were protests in Nigeria led by young people, some of whom were killed. Finding new political leadership that wants to remove these policy bottlenecks will be difficult, but I also don't think the status quo can preserve its privileges forever if the young generations stay engaged as checks on power.

Ibrahim Anoba

What Linda says is on point. Twenty, thirty, or forty years ago, you would not have seen the level of protest you saw in Nigeria. It's happened also in Cameroon, in Zambia, in Zimbabwe—protests unlike anything we've seen since the end of colonialism. This means that, as the populations change, social orientation towards the authority of governments is equally changing.

Brad Lips

Our friend Professor George Ayittey—the Ghanaian economist who last year published a great textbook with our Center for

African Prosperity, *Applied Economics for Africa*—has long talked about the idea of the "Cheetah Generation" rising up to replace a "Hippo Generation" that did not prioritize innovation and free markets. Is that wishful thinking or is that showing up in different ways? It's unfortunate that our Global Index of Economic Mentality has few data points from Africa at this stage, so it is not possible to make observations about the difference in viewpoints between young and old generations. Where do you see examples of disruptions from the Cheetah Generation?

Franklin Cudjoe

Well, there are private sector entrepreneurs creating wealth like George talks about as representing the Cheetah Generation, but with political change and policy change, it is difficult. Young people are venting on social media platforms across the continents. They often speak in terms that are not classical liberal, but they share discontent with governments that are corrupt and not responsive to public needs, so we need to work better to mobilize all the voices. Perhaps we engage them with "idea labs" associated with our think tanks to put forward new solutions.

Ibrahim Anoba

Yes, one thing we need to be candid about is that many of our peers in the Cheetah Generation do not understand the importance of liberal reform to the economy or the educational process. Even most of the folks involved directly in entrepreneurship, the Forbes 30 Under 30 set who could be drivers of the economy in Africa, have little or no awareness of the traditions in Africa and elsewhere of classical liberalism, and we need to engage these people in discussion of how to move our continent forward. Finding the intersection between our ideas and their ambitions is going to be critical to finding a workable path forward.

I hope we can do this because we do share the same goal—ending tyrannical or abusive states. The important point is that we cannot shy away from conversations with those who are not already studied in libertarianism. We desperately need to have these conversations and to be tactful, not leading with ideology, but earning trust because we share the goal of getting more freedom to people and thereby generating the prosperity the peoples of Africa deserve.

Brad Lips

Are the conversations also complicated by the reality that Africa, perhaps more than any other continent, has countries that are incredibly dissimilar, and even within particular countries, there are large numbers of different languages and cultures? Is it possible for a "Pan African Liberal Consciousness" to take root? Or do we need to think about the challenge in a very different way?

Linda Kavuka

Well, in my experience working with programs across the continent with Students for Liberty, I have come to believe we are more connected and more similar than we know. And when we get the chance to interact with each other, we find that we actually have just the same challenges.

Of course, since this is a community that's also studied the classical liberal ideas, we have a kind of shared vocabulary about solutions that then needs to be customized for our situations back home. It does get more challenging, as Ibrahim reminds us, that Marxist ideas have been engraved into the education systems in Africa and people just haven't been exposed to our ideas. We have a very daunting task to start from scratch and to work to bring people over to our views.

Trade for me is the easiest issue to get people thinking in a different way. Freedom in the abstract is difficult to appreciate if you're dealing with the living reality of hunger and poverty. Showing how removing very real barriers to trade can improve standards of living is a great place to begin these conversations, and then we can add to it in piecemeal ways.

Brad Lips

This seems a great place to talk about the Africa Continental Free Trade Area (AfCFTA) and the upside for a continent that includes twenty-seven of the thirty-nine countries ranked "unfree" in the *Economic Freedom of the World* report. AfCFTA has been billed as the largest free-trade area in the world, with a combined GDP of $3.3 trillion. One wonders whether some of Africa's countries could leap ahead like the Tiger economies of Hong Kong, Taiwan, and South Korea that opened to trade and boomed after 1960 or so. Am I overselling the potential here?

Franklin Cudjoe

Well, let's put Magatte on the spot. She has a lot of experience in this regard as an entrepreneur on the ground in this continent. I'm curious if this is opening up opportunities for vendors in different parts of Africa.

Magatte Wade

Thank you, Franklin. So before I start, I'm just going to say that I am always, always, always in favor of the free movement of people, goods, and ideas. Always. So from that standpoint this initiative is a positive one. Of course, as Ibrahim has written in his articles, everything really depends on how AfCFTA is implemented, and that's understandably an ongoing process.

As of right now, however, it is of no value to me and my business. I'll tell you why. My factory is in Senegal. To make our products, some ingredients we can find at the standard I need, in country. But the majority are not available in-country, and it has been a painstaking process to figure out how to source them and to get them on schedule and so on. While it's tempting to think I can go up and down my supply chain and find substitutes that might be marginally cheaper as trade rules improve, for a small- or medium-sized enterprise like mine, where quality assurance is the key dimension of my business, it's just impossible.

Multi-billion-dollar brands like Nike could likely do it, but it's hard enough for me to do what I do focusing on my core business and maintaining the quality I need. Of course, if I start asking, "Can you provide the packaging I need in this particular way?" my volumes right now don't justify making the changes they would need to make.

This is my problem. I still need what I need; the other African countries can't give it to me, because we have not industrialized. Why? Because the business environment is so crappy, so we get stuck in this cycle.

Something needs to break the cycle, and over time the AfCFTA could help if it leads to freedom of trade across Africa and the rest of the world. But in the near-term, I don't expect it to have a bearing for my entrepreneurial activities as I just have not found vendors in Africa that I would have the confidence to switch to.

Linda Kavuka

I really love this topic. The free-trade area was my focus for my master's thesis, so when I was writing that in 2019, I read the entire agreement at that time, and I'm very excited about the results that can come over time.

So here we are with all fifty-six African countries signing the agreement except Eritrea. We've chosen to house the free-trade area in Ghana, which was exciting. There is selecting the officials, which is going on now. But now the next step, which is the most important, is ratification so that the signatory countries are prepared to put free trade into practice. Of course, this is stirring up arguments within countries that traditionally have tried to close borders rather than open them, or that complain about outside products in their countries, and now they need to open up the entire continent. Nigeria closed off foreign imports of rice and chicken and meat, saying Nigerians should consume what is grown locally. What did it do for the Nigerian economy? Devaluation of the *naira*, and cost of living increasing to an extent it harms the everyday Nigerian. We need a change of attitudes with our governments in relation to trade, and this agreement will push countries toward these norms of trade.

COVID also slowed down the process of operationalizing the free-trade area, but there is still a lot of momentum. A lot of people are gaining expertise and lots of professionals are aligning themselves to be able to support businesses to operate across borders with the new openness.

Now, as Magatte alludes to, this is not a panacea since Africa lacks industrial capacity in various places, and also we have such underdeveloped infrastructure. You can imagine a road that might deliver a Kenyan coconut oil of the quality Magatte needs in Senegal, but of course this would require going straight through the Congo rainforest, and this is of course an area of near-constant civil unrest. So, yes, there are some challenges we have already been facing for years that are still there.

Ibrahim Anoba

Right. So first, Linda, if you will kindly please share your research with me, I would love to look at it. I'd like to add a little bit of historical dimension to the AfCFTA, because a lot of people look at it as a recent emergence or a recently conceived plan to address the contemporary problem, whereas this brings me back to Africa's own liberal free-trade tradition. Africans had been trading long before the continent was colonized. It's not like our forebears didn't know how to trade.

This dream of inter-African trade goes all the way back to the beginning of the 1900s when the Pan-African Congress was hosted in London, Westminster Hall. Surprisingly, the idea was championed quite prominently by the likes of W.E.B. Du Bois, who now is remembered as identifying with communism. In the middle of the twentieth century, the idea of free trade in Africa was developed by Kwame Nkrumah, who leaned toward the communist East block, given his focus on fighting imperialism. And then in 2005, it was Gaddafi in Libya, whom we disagreed with on so many things, who called for us to imagine a United States of Africa.

So that suggests to us that we should be open-minded and that strange bedfellows could help us achieve liberal goals. When thinking about value-creating enterprises, like Magatte described, I see it's not widely appreciated that a lot of African governments are now understanding how important small- and medium-sized enterprises are to the economy. Governments are increasingly incentivized to, for example, make it easier for businesses to get loans. They know local companies must compete all across Africa now. They know successful companies will create jobs and tax revenue and attract more foreign direct investment, so they finally have a stake in a part of society that was neglected in the past—a part of society where most people find their living. But one more point, which our friend Nathan Tjirimuje from Namibia makes and Dr. Ayittey shows in his *Applied Economics for Africa*, is that Africans can create our own savings and capital. We don't have to import capital to have capital. What we lack is not capital, per se, but freedom.

Moreover, capital should be free, like labor and services and goods, to travel to where it produces the greatest value. That means investors from Kenya being free to invest in Nigeria and Nigerians being free to invest in Ghana, and so on, and to work, offer services, and create a giant market that will increase the productivity of labor, of capital, and of ideas. And it's the freedom to find those opportunities and to be innovative that will increase their productivity.

Brad Lips

So a key is not just to allow goods to travel, but to realize the four freedoms that the European Union put at the heart of their economic zone? The free movement across borders of goods, capital, services, and labor?

Ibrahim Anoba

Well, yeah. And it means you'd better now prepare your local firms for free competition. So a lot of governments are now making loan processes much more accessible. In Nigeria, for instance, the local textile industry needs to learn to compete with, for example, the textile industry in Ghana, when the AfCFTA provisions actually come into play. So in that sense, it's really making government look, not only outward, but inward, as well, and asking how to free local firms to compete effectively.

The other exciting development is seeing trade as the basis of bilateral and multilateral relations in Africa, instead of war and military engagement. Previously, the only talk between Nigeria's leaders and those in Chad might have been about Boko Haram. Now the topic is AfCFTA and economic integration between the countries.

Brad Lips

Is the embrace of free trade also helping countries move past reliance on foreign aid? I love what Ghana's president said in December 2017: "We can no longer pursue a policy for our countries and regions that is based on the support given by the West . . . . This has not worked and it will not work."

Franklin Cudjoe

Yes, the move from aid to trade is happening for a number of countries on the continent. Foreign aid contributions in Ghana represent less than 1 percent of the country's GDP, and barely 3 percent of the government budget. Many are learning quite quickly that trade is the way to go, and the fundamental idea that we cannot be saved by donor countries sending aid seems to have garnered a lot more interest.

Since the UK opted out of the EU, it is now having a lot of bilateral trade deals with most African countries, and UK trade with Ghana will potentially be much greater than it used to be when they were part of the EU. That has begun to open the eyes of government officials to think not only of how to maximize opportunities with the West, but actually of how to deepen trade and economic freedom within the country as well.

Linda Kavuka

Allow me to note that COVID also disrupted the aid mentality in an interesting way. Governments had no option. COVID was coming and you needed supplies that you don't have. What do you do? In my country, Kenya, we saw temporary manufacturing pop up rather quickly to produce the PPE that doctors needed. Unfortunately, those reforms may have been only temporary, but I hope that what we take away from this period is an appreciation that we need R&D, technology, and innovation to be free to prepare for future challenges.

Ibrahim Anoba

I guess my biggest fear when it comes to COVID is how much will the government's power contract after COVID? They like those new emergency powers. So will they be willing to reopen the borders they closed? Will the central bank loosen the restrictions they have placed on accounts? The ability to monitor people for public health reasons, will this be temporary or not?

Franklin Cudjoe

Another topic that ties into some of our discussion is the role of the Chinese government, replacing aid agencies, in bringing resources for infrastructure projects. One lesson that few in Africa have come to terms with is that these deals are corrupt and usually not in our best interest. The deals get done practically overnight—suddenly you see roads being built—because the money arrives in bags rather than through the international financial system where there might be more accountability. So that is the template that is tough to resist when there is just more difficulty to get financing for infrastructure projects right now from sources in the West. Perhaps the great hope is that, if AfCFTA begins to succeed, traditional investors will compete to finance these projects, because they will see the promise of what Africa will look like if it is mostly middle class with a population of 2.4 billion people in 2050, as per these projections.

Brad Lips

Let's pivot to a related topic. In my discussion with your peers in the Asian liberty movement, we talked about the problem that China's economic growth seems to provide a model of capitalism that is directed by a repressive one-party state. Inside Africa, I suppose, Rwanda may present a similar story. After the genocide of 1994, its economic transformation has been quite miraculous, but we know that Paul Kagame has been ruthless toward political opposition.

Franklin Cudjoe

Yes, certainly a lot of what Kagame has done in Rwanda is getting them some mileage in terms of efficiency and on the *Doing Business* report, they are doing quite well. But beneath it all is a suppression of freedoms.

Magatte Wade

One of the troubling trends on the continent in our era is how certain governments—I certainly see it in the francophone countries of West Africa—are cracking down on civil society leaders who raise questions about elections or the propriety of seeking office for more terms than are legally mandated.

Ibrahim Anoba

I've seen a lot of Africanist professors talk about pursuing the Rwandan kind of model and making a connection to the idea that some of the most celebrated African ethnic kingdoms in history had a strong man at the helm of affairs. I think this is absolutely wrong; they're only looking at it from the standpoint of power, and not asking what allowed regular people to thrive and live in peace. So this is another conversation that we need to be careful about because we don't share the same underlying assumptions.

But again, let me come back to this idea of a Pan-African liberal consciousness. People may not categorize their mindset as liberal, but of course if you want human rights, if you want less interference in your daily life from fascist governments, you are some form of liberal whether you realize that or not.

Part of my current research is about many threads of the freedom philosophy that can be discovered in ancient Egyptian literature. You have people talking about tax rebellions because government is too burdensome. You have statements about respecting others' property and investing in your own. This consciousness has been in Africa for centuries, even millennia. So let's not be dissuaded from engaging in conversations with people who may not agree that they are liberal, because there is usually more common ground than we suspect.

Chapter Eleven

A Decade Since the Arab Spring

The countries of the Middle East and North Africa mostly tend to rank low on the Global Index of Economic Mentality. The Maghreb, the Levant, the Gulf States, and their neighbors share some common challenges but also many differences. Outsiders should keep in mind, among other things, that not all Arabs are Muslim; that most Muslims are not Arab; that not all inhabitants in the region speak Arabic; and that the region has a wide diversity of political systems. That said, the cultural and historical connections present a set of common problems and opportunities.

Since it has been a decade since the Arab Spring, I was especially excited to have a conversation about what Atlas Network partners have learned over the past ten years. How does the relationship between economic liberty and political reform play out in the region? Are there countries that provide a positive example in either sphere? Where should liberals in the region concentrate efforts to effect positive change?

To answer these and other questions, I convened a conversation in February 2021 about trends in the Middle East and North Africa with four thought leaders. *Kathya Berrada* is senior program manager at the Arab Centre for Scientific Research and Humane Studies in Rabat, Morocco. *Dr. Nouh El Harmouzi* is founder of the Arab Research Center and a professor of economics at Ibn Toufail University in Kenitra, Morocco. *Patrick Mardini* is the founding CEO of the Lebanon Institute for Market Studies and an assistant professor of finance at the University of Balamand. *Dr. Ali Salman* is based in Pakistan and serves as executive director of the Islam and Liberty Network, which runs educational programs in the MENA region and beyond.

Brad Lips

I'll start with a question for Nouh, who had the opportunity to address tens of thousands of the protesters in Cairo's Tahrir Square in April 2011 after the fall of Hosni Mubarak. My colleague Tom Palmer recorded an inspiring video of Nouh giving a short speech in Arabic, congratulating the Arab Spring protesters but also warning them not to submit to power, but to create a civilian state, ruled neither by theocrats nor by generals. Nouh, you warned, "Do not let the politicians steal your freedom. Free Egyptian people can create miracles." Ten years later, what are the lessons of the Arab Spring?

Nouh El Harmouzi

Reflecting back on the past ten years since the inception of the Arab Spring, we have learned the hard way that overthrowing a regime is easier than building a new system. This is clearly noticeable in the case of Tunisia, Libya, Syria, Yemen, as well as Egypt. We might agree on removing or changing what is in place, but building a new political system to replace it requires getting a majority of people to agree on viable solutions to everyday challenges and problems as experienced by the society at large. This last part is indeed more difficult to achieve.

A second point worth mentioning is that political progress does not always translate into economic and social progress. This is clearly the case of Tunisia and somewhat in Morocco and Jordan too. A societal transition that has lasting positive effects cannot take place without a clear road map that has a certain level of agreement among many of the stakeholders in society.

The next point is that revolutions don't always bring transitions to greater democracy. We need to keep in mind that since the end of the Second World War, there have been roughly fifty revolutions worldwide, but only a third of these revolutions led to democracy. Moreover, democracy building requires more than elections to succeed. It also needs informed citizens, a common set of rules, and acceptance that political pluralism and divergent views are part of the democratic process. In the case of the Arab Spring, we were not able to develop a solid institutional framework to fill the vacuum that followed revolution.

Ali Salman

Yes, the Islam Liberty Network that I run was actually founded in 2011, so we are turning ten along with the Arab Spring. An upcoming seminar will explore these exact issues as they have played out in Tunisia, Morocco, and Algeria. We all remember that the first trigger point of the Arab Spring was the self-immolation of a man named Mohamed Bouazizi, a street vendor who committed suicide in protest of all the corruption and exploitation that made his daily struggle to earn a living unbearable. Our team looked into whether, in the last ten years, in Tunisia specifically, the government has made any reforms to make the economy more inclusive for street vendors like Bouazizi.

Instead of creating bottom-up opportunities through economic reform, the government is following a statist paradigm of diagnosing this as a problem of unemployment that should be solved by government creation of jobs. This seems to be the wrong direction.

On the other hand, in terms of democracy, Tunisia offers a good example for the rest of the Arab world. While almost all Tunisians, maybe 99 percent, are Muslims, there is a lot of pluralism in terms of interpretations of Islam. The way Tunisia reconciled different views of Islam into the new constitution which they came up with is admirable and inspiring, in my opinion. This is why it is worrisome that the general understanding of economic freedom is very poor at the moment. If they can't get the economy right, despite their good intentions, then frustrations will increase and maintaining a successful democratic transition will be more difficult.

Kathya Berrada

Thinking retrospectively, ten years ago, I was still a student back in France, and I was extremely enthusiastic about the whole Arab Spring movement. Certainly, with hindsight it is easier to be more nuanced and prudent in my appreciation. Foremost, street protests, no matter how genuine they are, cannot be substitutes for true civic and political engagement.

A second lesson is that, in trying to assess the way forward in different countries, we cannot simply rely on officially reported aggregated macroeconomic data, which often hide much more complicated realities. This was the case, for instance, in Tunisia and to some extent also in Egypt where macroeconomic indicators and especially growth rate before the inception of the Arab Spring looked promising, but actually did not give us a true picture of the socio-economic challenges facing ordinary citizens. They instead masked a reality of exclusion, absence of true middle classes and socio-economic fragilities.

Brad Lips

Patrick, I'm also interested in how these reflections on the Arab Spring protests sound from your perspective, as someone who's seen, rather recently, sizable protests in the streets of Lebanon.

Patrick Mardini

The common element across all those protests that gave birth to the Arab Spring and to the protests in Lebanon is the bad economic conditions. The message was clear: the bad economic conditions are the consequence of corruption. Those are the words you hear: declining opportunity, increasing prices, because of corruption. However, there were some difficulties in having a clear path to prosperity. It's easy to identify the problem, but it's a different matter to design a solution to get you out of this problem after the protests end.

What seems clear to me is that government intervention in the economy is the tool for all the corruption that people are protesting against. If you are government and you want to stay in power, you increase the size of the public sector—not just police and army, but the role of government in the economy—so that more people will be beholden to you. Corruption and totalitarianism go hand in hand with bigger government. That's for sure. That's what we can see in our region. Also, those same people enrich themselves through public tenders. They do contracts of the government-owned companies with their cronies. So you would hire a company to build new electricity factories and instead of costing a billion Lebanese pounds, it will be priced at five billion and the difference will be kickbacks to enrich this political class.

The solution is easy in principle: install economic freedom so the government isn't in a position to determine economic outcomes across society, and the politicians aren't in a position to enrich themselves at the public's expense.

Brad Lips
Of course, that's easier said than done, especially in a region that has many low-scoring countries on the Global Index of Economic Mentality. Tunisia and Egypt are among the ten lowest scores, and Lebanon itself ranks fifty-nine of the seventy-nine countries for which we have data at present.

Patrick Mardini
Indeed, it is a big problem, and what people still do not understand is that it is futile to just change the regime without changing the underlying economic causes of society's problems. You will get back into a bad situation where the leader either falls to a revolt or becomes dictatorial to stay

in power. So, solving the underlying economic problem can provide not only a path to prosperity but also a path to democracy.

Now, about how we tackle the challenge of increasing appreciation for economic freedom. That is our *raison d'être* as a free-market think tank.

We need to resolve this general idea—government intervention is the cause of the problem, and the solution for your problem is less government intervention—into specific problems to solve. Like why does Lebanon have a problem with unreliable and unaffordable electricity? Well, because the government is managing electricity. We must make the counterintuitive case that to solve this problem we need less government spending on electricity. Governments must allow entrepreneurs the space to solve the problems that government cannot efficiently address. It is counterintuitive to explain that problems can be solved without a specific plan for government action, but that's our job. We do need, though, to present plans to eliminate state monopolies and to create the legal framework and rules within which voluntary action can solve the problems where governments have failed.

Kathya Berrada
One point I would like to add is that, yes, a major problem in our region is that economic and political power are often intertwined and usually concentrated in the hands of a small number of people, generally close to or within the ruling circles. This obvious collusion takes place to sustain and nourish the same ruling elite, and this is very dangerous.

Because, let's face it, investors will be very averse to invest when they know that the competing company next to them is owned by the ruling dynasty or by someone close to or within the military power. This hazardous concentration of political and economic powers in the hands of the same close circle has not been addressed enough in the major discussions that we hear about in the Arab world. The negative impacts of this situation on economic freedom are very clear.

Now, thinking about our approach to increase appreciation of economic freedom, let me comment on our programs at the Arab Centre for Research which is based in Morocco, but which has programs across the MENA region.

Our core teaching and outreach programs always emphasize the importance of both political and economic institutions in getting people moving toward prosperity. They have become increasingly multi-disciplinary; we emphasize linkages between, on the one side, rule of law and economic principles, and more practical topics like refugees' integration and women's rights. We want to help people understand how economic empowerment and political empowerment best go hand in hand.

Nouh El Harmouzi

When I think about the causes of the aversion to liberal ideas in our region, there are some that may be common with other developing countries and some that may be specific to us. Generally, many people see a "cult of the market" that pits the wallet against the heart. They see rule-based competition that rewards winners and hurts losers with no room for generosity or no sense of public solidarity. In this context, those who promise government intervention on behalf of the large masses come across as nice people. This happens in many places that are poor or developing.

What might be specific to our region is a cultural sense that we need a strong leader or a strong state or strong providence to protect us from an imperial external enemy that today shows up as multinational firms. Another factor may be that the dominant religion in this MENA region is Islam, which turned, after its golden age in the eleventh century, to an interpretation that gives much political power to an imam, whom we need to obey. That gives less room for innovation and principles that are important to liberal and free-market societies.

Ali Salman

Thank you, Nouh, for pointing this out. I agree that this is how it has been, but let's talk about today. I'd say that the question that we actually used for the first Islam Liberty Network meeting in 2011 is outdated. We were asking whether Islam and democracy were compatible.

Let's consider the last couple of decades, measuring liberalism in political terms, in economic terms, and in religious terms. Interestingly, when we organized our fifth ILN international conference it was in Malaysia, which at the time was in democratic transition. And one of the main themes from that conference was this question about compatibility between Islam and democracy. Outside of some pockets of violence, most Muslim-majority countries—Malaysia, Indonesia, Turkey, Bangladesh, Pakistan—have mostly adopted democracy as a system of governance, albeit with many flaws. So there is a degree of acceptance of more liberal interpretations of Islam as pro-democracy.

Where we have more fundamental problems is in terms of economic liberties and also—the hardest one—religious liberties. With economics, you can say that Turkey moved in a positive direction nearly two decades ago and has shown the results of that economic opening. Malaysia too. So we do have some mostly positive examples to follow and to learn from.

As Patrick has pointed out, much of the problem is about corruption. In this way, I would point out it's not an interpretation of Islam that is affecting economic mentality but the lived experience people have with their governments. Also, the secular intellectuals who are most influential in our societies also are under the influence of socialist ideology. They may not be following Islam in their public views, but they still favor a big state and are opposed to open trade and competition. There are multiple challenges which we face.

Patrick Mardini

I'd like to add two points to this discussion. The first point is that we have been living with nationalist socialist governments in the region—in Syria, in Egypt, in Libya, and so on. All those dictatorships were actually socialist, and they engaged in massive brainwashing, shaking their fingers at capitalism and equating it with imperialism. So our battle is against thirty or more years of accumulated misinformation. My second point is that we need to be intentional in our language and strategies. For instance, I say, "I am against privatization," because, in our context, privatization was a means of corruption. Politicians hand the telecom industry to a friend and let him manage it as a monopoly. Since privatization is equated with corruption, it is the last thing I would focus on. I say instead, "Open the market to competition. Allow for new companies to come in. Don't privatize what you want to keep. At least not now. The first step is to open the market."

Another point is that we should look at the half-full part of the glass, because we have been looking at the empty part. If you look at the Gulf countries—United Arab Emirates, Dubai, et cetera—they have been producing a lot of prosperity to their citizens. In Dubai, you don't have oil, so they thrive by being an open city, with predictable rule of law, low taxation. It is quite a contrast with the nationalist socialist regimes that have produced poverty and corruptions. It provides an example of how a conservative Muslim community, deeply attached to their faith, can also be prosperous with economic freedom.

Ali Salman

There are a few reasons to see Dubai as an outlier, and perhaps difficult to take as an example that can be applied more broadly. Dubai's population is very small; there is a much higher concentration of ex-pats than really anywhere else in the region.

Nouh El Harmouzi
Yes, Dubai was fortunate to confront the problem of running out of oil much earlier than others, which has been a true impetus to economic diversification. Other Gulf countries continue to believe they still have oil to rely upon as a source of national income. The last point to keep in mind is that after the financial crisis of 2008, Dubai required significant money from Abu Dhabi. Without it, I don't think that we would have the Dubai of today.

Patrick Mardini
I still would make the case that Dubai might be less of an outlier than the beginning of a certain positive trend, as we see places like Qatar following its path. And even if it is an outlier, I would say that it's a nice pilot study. It's not a perfect free-market ideal—there is lots of government intervention in the economy through construction projects, and that is really the bubble that burst, leading to bailouts, but that happened in many economies, including the US. To touch on what Ali raised, yes, Dubai has attracted many immigrants who come there to work, but this is fabulous, right? This is real proof of how a free-market economy can bring together different races, different religions, people who don't know each other, who are very different from each other, to cooperate willingly in a productive way without central planning for that. I think that's admirable.

Brad Lips
While we're talking about the Gulf States, let me get your perspectives on a big event of the fall of 2020: the Abraham Accords that normalized relations between Israel and some

of the Gulf States and some parts of North Africa. Have the Accords been oversold or underappreciated in your estimation?

Kathya Berrada

I will speak mostly from the Moroccan experience. We are in the midst of what we call here in Morocco "re-establishment" of the relationship with Israel, instead of the more common "normalization" term used in other parts of the Arab World. Morocco and Israel normalized relations more than twenty years ago by the openings of respective diplomatic representations. The process was nevertheless suspended for a period of time following conflicts in Gaza. I am very pro-normalization of the relationship, as I deeply believe that cooperation, trade, and dialogue are more conducive to stability and prosperity.

It is difficult to say whether the Abraham Accords were oversold or undersold. This is a marathon and not a sprint, and it is only starting, but the prospects are good. We can expect economic and scientific collaboration. Morocco and Israel both face challenges when it comes to water scarcity, climate change, and renewable energies, which constitute good starting points for cooperation. Last, but not least, Morocco has a significant Jewish community. According to folks, the Jewish presence in Morocco traces back its origin as early as the first destruction of the Temple.

Patrick Mardini

In the past, when Arab states signed peace deals with Israel, there was no real uptick of trade that happened in its wake. This time, there is a good chance it will be different. I look at it as new markets opening up to each other. Each one of those places is able to specialize in a different way, and then they can trade. It can bring a substantial prosperity if this happens—which, of course, we will only know with the passage of time—but certainly these trading relationships could bring normal peace.

Nouh El Harmouzi

I totally agree with what was said, but let's keep in mind that we have two competing and divergent discourses. From one side, we have the official normalization, but not what I call the "street normalization." If you talk to many Egyptians, they will say, "No, they normalized," meaning the politicians, "but we did not." This indicates that normalization with Israeli is not always endorsed by the populations.

So I would say the law and politicians are ahead of the general population. There is a big gap here. It will take time, but as my colleagues said, it is a positive development that could be coming slowly and gradually.

Brad Lips

This relates to what I wanted to raise next. If the challenge is to get more of the population in the region to be included in the market economy, what are the levers for change? What opportunities do you want to unleash to create the social mobility and inclusivity that we associate with economically free countries?

Ali Salman

I'd return again to the project of street vendors that I mentioned at the beginning. We need to focus on problems of livelihood that resonate with the public. There is great sympathy on this issue, so we gain greatly if we show how serious problems can be solved from an economically liberal point of view.

Kathya Berrada

Yes, a challenge in this part of the world is rebutting the idea that market economy is about making the rich richer and not caring for the poor. In our intellectual kind of discussions, we can rebut these misrepresentations easily, but those discussions remain limited in their reach, and more efforts are needed to get the message to larger parts of the society.

As liberals in the Arab world, we need to tackle socio-economic issues and make it clear that we prioritize them. We need Arab populations to hear us say, "We hear your problems, and those are real problems. Our way of addressing poverty is simply different, and I think better. It is not through government intervention but through economic freedom and the entrepreneurship and dynamism that is directly linked to it." Too often, our small liberal community has seemed content to ignore the elephant in the room, which makes people think that somehow we have no interest in the core issues of poverty and unemployment.

Patrick Mardini

Lebanon is going though one of the harshest economic crises in its history. The GDP of Lebanon is estimated to have dropped from $52 billion in 2019 to $18 billion in 2020. That's not 50 percent. That's not 60 percent. That's more like 65 percent. It is a huge shrinkage of the economy and now more than half of the population is under the poverty line.

The human suffering is overpowering, but this is not a time for despair but for us to promote solutions. Media exposure for the Lebanese Institute for Market Studies has skyrocketed. Everyone wants information on the economy and this is our specialization. [We've gone] from three interviews per week to twenty-six per week. People are open to our ideas as we say, "What you're doing has been wrong. You need to liberate and de-cronyize the economy."

Our initiatives are getting traction: to move to cash transfers for the poor (very close to a universal basic income) instead of subsidizing goods, which is very inefficient; to stop inflation by bringing discipline to the central bank via a currency-board solution, which we are promoting with Dr. Stephen Hanke; and to continue our work on electricity, which already achieved some reforms. On the last, we are working toward a future in which private companies can build, operate, and manage electricity infrastructure without government intervention. And we are proposing more reforms in water, freedom to trade, and more.

Brad Lips

Let's stay on Lebanon for another minute. In a year of shocks, the explosion at the port of Beirut was one of the more shocking moments of 2020. What lessons were learned from that disaster?

Patrick Mardini

What I think was most incredible, and encouraging, in the wake of this tragedy was what people in the street told Emmanuel Macron when he visited a month after the explosion. They were shouting, "Don't give money to the politicians." People were against an instant relief program. Can you imagine that? This is impressive that people, very much in need, saw that their plight would not be helped by giving money to the government, as it would only be stolen by the politicians and cronies.

Of course, the most important point of the port explosion is how it highlighted the corruption of policy makers. Everyone looked the other way and no one was responsible. A private company would have never stored explosive fertilizer material—for free—amid the most expensive real estate in Lebanon. They would have used it in a more efficient way. We have said this for a long time, and now we are saying that we should not have the government manage the port anymore. The private sector can do faster reconstruction anyway, and competition among the ports in Lebanon will improve the economy.

Brad Lips

Let's take our last minutes together to pan out and take a wider view. For liberal think tanks in the MENA region, where will you be trying to make an impact over the next five to ten years?

Ali Salman

One of the indicators of success that I want to see improve is the level of engagement with the politicians. I was very pleased at Patrick's success with MPs wanting to hear him and Steve Hanke testify on the currency board solution. That is a good example of what it looks like if we can up our game as think tanks. We should all be proud of the work we do through media and public engagement, but getting the attention of the politicians—who follow, as we know, the most popular ideas—is where we need more impact.

To reflect briefly on our post-COVID situation, we especially need to convince the political class that the emergency powers they have grabbed—this heightened atmosphere of government intervention—should not become part of a permanent policy. Lots of work is needed in this direction.

Nouh El Harmouzi

At the Arab Center our operational framework is twofold. The practical actions are very important, but we embrace the long game of changing minds through books and articles, podcasts, intellectual engagement, and events. I mean, Adam Smith's *Wealth of Nations*, if you had measured its impact ten years after it was published I'm not sure what you would have found. But after one hundred years, the scale of its influence was tremendous.

As such, we prioritize publishing the kinds of works—like our Arabic translation of Tom Palmer's *The Morality of Capitalism*—that can clarify the difference between entrepreneurial capitalism and crony capitalism, since this is a fundamental confusion that impedes economic progress in our countries.

On the practical side, in the wake of COVID-19 we see an opportunity to work toward greater regional economic integration. We just had a meeting with analysts at the World Bank. The statistics are pretty astounding. Our region has 64 percent of its trade with Europe and the US, but only 16 percent of trade is intra-regional. We need to work more on finding synergies within this region.

It is a good time for this topic because of some new thinking coming out after COVID. It is kind of strange for us to suddenly have many establishment organizations—the World Bank, the International Monetary Fund, McKinsey, the World Economic Forum—all talking about the importance of entrepreneurship in the context of "The Great Reset." I am extremely happy to read that they are coming to our solutions after years of being critical. They talk of stakeholder capitalism, instead of shareholder capitalism, so we certainly have things to say about that. But broadly, we should be encouraged they are agreeing that economies will be driven by entrepreneurship.

Kathya Berrada
In addition to focusing on the demand side, where we want to create interest in our ideas and solutions, we try also to increase the supply side by equipping civil society actors with the skills to contribute to public policy processes.

For example, we're running a program in Turkey which looks specifically at the integration of refugees from a non-state-agent perspective. We're looking at the role of private sectors. We're looking at the role of faith groups. We're looking at the role of civil society organizations in integrating refugees. It seems more effective to take very practical topics and try to analyze them from a liberal mindset that finds solutions rather than calling for a top-down initiative by government.

Since the Arab Center is a regional organization, one of the major achievements for us is that we provide a space for different actors from the Arab region—with different backgrounds, some religious and some nonreligious—to come together and exchange ideas.

The next frontier for us as a think tank is to take this special community we have brought together and do more to bridge the gap between the academic and intellectual leaders and those in policy-making roles.

Patrick Mardini

What we're all working for is to have better standards of living everywhere. As Lebanon is in a crisis, the success I want is to reduce the poverty that is especially caused by hyperinflation and currency devaluation. People make their income in the Lebanese pound, and inflation means they become poorer and poorer. If we can stop the vicious cycle, that by itself is a fantastic achievement.

Moreover, as we collect examples of what actually works, we can promote those solutions in many places that have similar problems. You have currency devaluation in Sudan right now, in Turkey from time to time. If we're able to produce a solution that works in Lebanon, we can export it to other places. This is a long-term vision.

We need to become reliable sources of effective policy solutions. I would include climate change in this conversation. It is likely to become a more important problem, and if we leave the field for the socialists and communists to develop solutions, the problems will likely multiply. That's an area where I would like to see more work by free-market thinkers. In the meantime, we have our clear goals for change in Lebanon, and of course we have key performance indicators to help us see whether we are on the right track. Media exposure is an obvious place we measure our performance, because it's a market signal that our work has value.

Nouh El Harmouzi

Yes, I wish to reiterate how I agree with Patrick's framework of measuring the impact of our efforts in both qualitative and quantitative ways. As Kathya pointed out, part of our efforts at the Arab Center have been to develop civil society actors who can take this message, build their own organizations, and achieve important things on their own.

Brad Lips

Yes, this last point about the value of a real network brings us full circle to a comment you made at the beginning—that the Arab Spring proved that we need more stakeholders who care about liberty and justice and peace and that we need more connectedness among them. Our network started from a small base many years ago, which is why everyone is so impressed and thrilled by the progress being made, thanks to the efforts of all of you in this discussion and those of your many colleagues and partners.

Section 3

A Path Forward for Liberalism
and the Free Society

Chapter Twelve
A Path Forward

By the time 2020 staggered to its close, it had become passé to bemoan the year in which nothing seemed to go right.

The COVID-19 pandemic and its disruptions were the center of the story, but there were other subplots: an ugly US presidential campaign leading to a contested election outcome and violence, tragic instances of police brutality answered by a mix of legitimate protests and looting and arson. The rulers of Russia and China stepped up their assaults on liberal democracy, and the world experienced a bevy of natural disasters, including locust swarms in Africa, murder hornets in the United States, and wildfires that wreaked havoc in Australia and California.

We're talking dysfunction of biblical proportions.

Of course, while we now may harbor nostalgia for the simpler days of 2019, we were not problem-free entering the COVID era. As discussed in the six regional conversations included in this book, around the world we see rising authoritarianism, extreme public debt burdens, risks of monetary instability, and weakening trust in liberal democracy and the rule of law. Those challenges remain.

They are compounded now by what is unprecedented in our lifetimes: the task of bouncing back from a global pandemic. We should be mindful, however, that today's situation is not unprecedented in human history.

We might take some inspiration from the events of one hundred years ago. While America had been ravaged by the Spanish Flu, World War 1, and abuses of civil liberties under Woodrow Wilson, 1921 marked a return to normalcy in the United States. Historian Amity Shlaes has noted that the 1920s were an optimistic era that saw class differences recede, a decline in racist incidents, and a creative culture renaissance. Much of that progress was attributable to a revival of the idea that governments should have limited powers and live within their means, trusting free people to cooperate and innovate through civic association and the free economy.

"Prosperity is a good healer," Shlaes said during Atlas Network's 2020 Liberty Forum, drawing a comparison between the 1920s and 2020s. "We need vaccines, but we need prosperity just as much."

Are there reasons to believe the 2020s could, in fact, bring a renaissance of progress? The answer is certainly yes.

No one should ignore how blessed we are to be taking our trips around the sun at this point in history. Pockets of poverty and oppression persist, but much of humanity has access to wonders that were unavailable to the richest monarchs of previous ages—modern pharmaceuticals, omnipresent potable water, a global communications network, refrigerated food sourced from all over the globe . . . . The list goes on and on.

Yes, the pandemic exposed serious flaws in the world's health infrastructure, but we can be grateful to have avoided the almost 3 percent global death rate of the Spanish Flu. That would have meant more than *230 million deaths* from COVID, rather than the 3.5 million figure the World Health Organization published at the end of May 2021. By that time, of course, COVID-19 vaccines had been developed, approved for public use, and rolled out in many countries—truly a miracle of modern science.

We also are fortunate to live in an era when deaths from violent causes—genocides, wars, homicide—are near historic lows.

World poverty rates, while ticking up during COVID, also are remarkably low compared to just a couple decades ago.

Equally remarkable, we now have hit a tipping point where our environmental footprints are getting lighter even as economic growth increases. Andrew McAfee's recent book, *More from Less*, tours the effects of "dematerialization"—the technology-fueled phenomenon that sees economic growth being accompanied by absolute declines in resource consumption. The important implication is that a clean and healthy environment and technological and economic progress need not be in opposition.

Good news abounds. Whether you're talking about life expectancy, conservation of natural habitats, access to clean water, women's rights, or ending hunger, the statistical trends have moved in very positive directions over the last four decades.

Boom or Doom?

So which is it? Are we living in the best of times or the worst of times?

I'm an optimist who sees our world on the cusp of very exciting decades of progress— *so long as we don't undermine the values that sustain liberal democracy*.

Among those values are a respect for the dignity of all people, a "live and let live" attitude that allows for pluralism, and the wisdom to hesitate to use the force of law for most situations. Frighteningly, here in the United States at least, those norms are increasingly under attack. We are becoming a safety-obsessed society that's unwilling to face the fact that all risks involve trade-offs. We are dangerously indebted but scared to make prudent changes to our spending trajectory. We distrust the same government institutions that we vote to expand and empower. We're so invested in the "narratives" of our different tribes that we tune out facts or try to silence opinions that don't validate pre-existing beliefs.

I'm no defeatist, but there is a crisis of values in America today. It's a crisis that can only be solved by rebuilding a consensus around the institutions of liberalism and the free society, and by renewing the culture of tolerance and personal responsibility.

What Is at Stake?

Most of the consequences of losing freedom are impossible to envision. What we could lose are the innovations that *would have been* born from the processes of trial and error that *would have happened* if people had had the freedom to innovate. Such innovations originate almost exclusively in free countries.

Ten years ago, few among us appreciated the enormous ripple effects of innovations in extracting energy from locations where it once seemed impossible. Fracking reduced energy costs for consumers, turned the United States into an exporter of fossil fuels, and altered geopolitics by draining the resources of illiberal oil-rich regimes.

Other changes have been more subtle but touch our lives all the same. Uber, Etsy, Airbnb and other new platforms of the gig economy have provided millions of people with more choices and greater flexibility for work and play. Telecommuting and telemedicine allow people to live where they want and avoid traffic congestion. We have an ever-widening abundance of choices in our days: on-demand entertainment of all stripes, exotic cuisines delivered to our doors, instant visual communication with loved ones in different countries—none of this was inevitable. They are the fruits that grew from the seeds of liberty.

It's worth pointing out that none of these amazing developments were driven by foresighted government officials. If anything, government officials most often opposed the very innovations I've identified. Rather than enabling the remote work that makes suburban and rural living attractive, governments invested in urban planning to increase living density. Rather than celebrating the gig economy, governments have tried to saddle innovators with labor regulations that undermine flexible work arrangements.

As ever, we see the tension between the top-down visions of so many government experts and the bottom-up manner in which progress typically emerges. The latter depends on having a system of economic liberty that rewards innovators who take risks to develop and market new processes, new products, and new services.

When we look back at how the US government erred in handling COVID-19 in 2020, the first mistake was the overreliance on the authority of bureaucrats at the Food and Drug Administration (FDA) and the Centers for Disease Control and Prevention (CDC). Those agencies prevented others from developing tests that might have limited the early spread of the virus. They bet on their own ability to solve a complicated problem from the top-down, and they failed to deliver. Taiwan and Korea took the opposite strategy, and public health benefited greatly.

I don't want to be doctrinaire in suggesting all government action is counterproductive. Having effective COVID vaccines before the end of 2020 was an incredible achievement, and while the federal government's Operation Warp Speed was not its lone catalyst, it played a productive role by providing regulatory green lights and guarantees of purchases of huge numbers of vaccine doses. In this situation, the Trump administration wisely let private actors compete for the business, rather than repeating its earlier mistake in letting a government agency control the R&D process concerning COVID testing.

Across the country, we saw state governments implement lockdowns of varying degrees. Some of that was prudent (e.g., the original effort to "flatten the curve" to reduce the chances of overwhelming hospitals with a rapid spread of the virus). Much of it, however, now seems misguided; by mandating that everyone take the same measures to minimize risks of one adverse outcome, governments failed to factor in the other risks that many people must also navigate.

Again, what seems most inspiring from the experience of 2020 is how remarkably people adapted when they had the freedom to do so. Restaurateurs pivoted to outdoor and ventilated dining, ditching communal menus for QR codes. Many private schools innovated fast to keep children learning, and parents rallied to create learning pods. Professional sports leagues moved to bubbles and pioneered the use of rapid tests to allow successful seasons to take place.

The lesson I take from 2020 is that resilience—the grit and ingenuity that keeps things working in a community—cannot be ordered from the top down.

The best we can do is provide a reliable governing framework that allows its emergence from the bottom up.

No doubt, there are new, difficult-to-predict challenges that await us in the future. To endure and overcome these challenges, we need innovators and risk-takers. We need citizens to be engaged at the local level and looking out for the vulnerable in their communities. We need the institutions of liberal democracy.

If those institutions erode instead, then our children and grandchildren will be less prepared for COVID-style Black Swan events that stress our institutions.

One of the biggest threats is no Black Swan because it is entirely too predictable. We have known for decades that the retirement of the Baby Boomer generation would stress, if not bankrupt, the existing Medicare and Social Security systems, but our political class never made responsible reforms. As these programs drain increasing percentages of the federal budget, the question that remains is whether the United States will be able to continue borrowing debt at historically low rates. If there is a comeuppance on the horizon—in the form of hyperinflation or sudden cuts to non-essential programs—the economic pain will be most deeply experienced by those with the fewest resources.

This might not be all.

Manuel Hinds's wonderful new book, *In Defense of Liberal Democracy*, examines how societies are tested during periods of disruption. Societies going through major technological changes (as we are now) are prone to unrest, and when economic crises arise in their midst, what might appear as sturdy institutional foundations can shake and fracture. Authoritarians can exploit such moments when politics already are divisive and all-consuming, preventing people from seeing the many dimensions through which even ideological enemies should be able to cooperate. In this context, elected leaders will be tempted to exploit their temporary power in ways that undo liberal institutions.

Resisting those authoritarian impulses is the duty of all genuine liberals, whether or not the people in power are committed to aspects of our own preferred policy agenda.

But this task takes some courage in the United States of 2021. As discussed in the chapter, "Land of the Free, Home of the Brave?" the threat of cancel culture undermines the ability to have free-flowing debates about important issues. This is compounded by a culture of risk aversion and deference to government authorities.

Those cultural trends, along with the progressive tilt to most education, may be behind a notable result in the Global Index of Economic Mentality—that the younger generation in the United States trails the older generation in their appreciation of economic freedom by a bigger margin than anywhere else in the world. That finding tracks with other survey data that have consistently shown that American millennials (born 1981–1996) and

members of Generation Z (born 1997–2012) are more favorable to socialism than capitalism.

From a global perspective, we can take some solace in more positive trends in other countries. For example, Estonia has an even larger gap between the GIEM scores of young and old, but its trend is flipped with the youth being the more free-market cohort.

But I am going to continue this chapter with a focus on the United States, which is the country I know best, and which I believe has an outsized responsibility to keep the faith with prior generations who gave their lives for the principles of a free society.

I remember the first gala dinner of Atlas Network that I ever attended, celebrating our organization's twentieth anniversary in San Francisco. Our keynote speaker was Walter Williams, the George Mason University economics professor and syndicated columnist who passed away in December 2020. He closed his speech on a solemn note:

> Our job as Americans is very, very crucial. That is, we have an awesome responsibility on us to preserve liberty. Because if liberty dies in the United States, it is my opinion, that it's gone everywhere, all over the world, forever.

In the Nob Hill event hall where Williams delivered this stark warning, there was immediate applause and our chairman, Bill Sumner, adroitly moved on to the next item in our program's agenda. But in my mind, a question lingered. It's a question that haunts me still.

What would it look like if the light of freedom were to die out?

Would it be how imprisoned publisher Jimmy Lai described his home town of Hong Kong in late 2020? Describing life since the once-vibrant pro-democracy movement was forcibly removed from the streets, Jimmy remarked: "It is peaceful now. But the silence is the silence of suffocation."

Or would the end of liberal democracy in the United States take the shape of violence? From the Jacobins of eighteenth-century France to so many Marxist movements of the last century, those who profess to have noble ideals can be impatient with dissenters who don't fall in line with the new agenda. The temptation of the guillotine is never far away.

The stakes, certainly, are high. So are the tensions and resentments that were exacerbated by the events of January 6, 2021.

Most Americans have strong feelings about the perfect storm of political strife we have just endured, so I'll do my best to recount— while avoiding political bias—recent American history, as simply as I can. My telling of the story goes like this:

Donald Trump was an unconventional president who defied many norms of etiquette and tradition. He drew energy from battling his enemies in politics and the media. Those enemies often strayed out of bounds them-selves, promoting unfounded conspiracies and unwittingly giving Trump the ammunition he needed to proclaim himself a victim of arrogant and powerful elites. Sincere criticisms and thoughtful defenses of the record of the Trump administration tended to be lost in the media maelstrom.

The presidential election of November 2020 happened under strange circumstances and yielded unusual results. Trump claimed there was widespread election fraud, but did not provide evidence to back up his claims. Trump's critics dismissed the possibility of irregularities with so little curiosity that it produced protests in Washington DC that spilled into an outrageous violation of the Capitol building that delayed the official certification of the election. Trump's actions leading up to the riot were typically unpresidential. Democrats and media elites responded with little magnanimity; in the end, the former president was impeached (for the second time) and stripped of his social media accounts.

All of this has created a level of social strife and political risk that's certainly not unique in the world, but is unprecedented for the United States during the post-Cold War era. Given the mistrust and yawning divides between different groups of Americans, I worry that another unexpected crisis could tear the fragile fabric of our freedoms.

This is why we need conversations around the emerging political realignment taking place in the United States, and we need to do it without resigning ourselves to failure. Below, I make the case that a different alignment is achievable—an alignment that could unite people of good will, Democrats, Republicans, Independents, Libertarians, Greens, and others, around common values.

I hope the analysis is instructive for other countries as well. The vision I outline is certainly not proprietary to any culture, as it appeals to the better angels of a universal human nature.

The New Political Realignment

The election of President Donald Trump in November 2016 and the United Kingdom's Brexit vote of five months earlier were earthquakes to a political status quo that was primed for a shake up. Commentators began to draw connections between the populist movement in the US and UK and political events in other countries that had shattered the elite consensus. President Recep Erdoğan in Turkey had consolidated his power while blasting a secular "deep state." The recently elected prime minister of India, Narendra Modi, led a new Hindu nationalist movement into power. In Europe, nationalist political parties rode to power, in part, by responding to anxiety about Muslim immigrants streaming out of war-torn Syria. In Mexico and Brazil governments were rocked by scandals and were ripe to be swept away in 2018 by outsiders.

While it's tempting to look at the surge of populism in the mid-to-late 2010s as a novel development, I am persuaded by the histo-rian Stephen Davies that the rise of populism is best understood as a symptom of a rather normal political realignment that we should expect to occur in democracies every forty years or so, when "the one or two major issues that define political identities and divisions change," (Davies, "The Great Realignment: Understanding Politics Today," *Cato Unbound*).

For most of my fifty years on this planet, political affiliations in the United States could be understood by the questions sketched out in this 2x2 matrix:

Political Alignments, 1970-2015

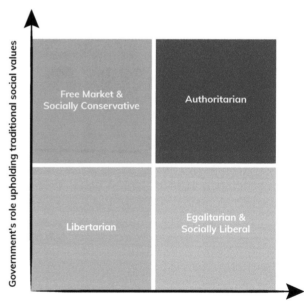

Government's role upholding traditional social values

Free Market & Socially Conservative

Authoritarian

Libertarian

Egalitarian & Socially Liberal

Government's role in economic outcomes

This is a simplified narrative, of course. Foreign policy issues were ascendant in some election cycles, and neither Democrats nor Republicans have practiced limited government as much as they preached it in their respective social and economic spheres. But the two major parties clearly branded themselves along these lines, so you could predict with some confidence that people in the red quadrant voted Republican, and people in the blue voted Democrat. Almost no American would show up in the authoritarian square, and, while self-identified "libertarians" are a vanishingly small community, lots of independents would self-identify as "economically conservative and socially liberal," making this purple square a pretty influential swing vote.

This description of America's political alignment made sense for more than four decades after the Vietnam War, but it no longer holds today. Looking at the emerging alignment that's taking place now, Davies has written that the social values question has been replaced by one that's really about "cultural identity." Are you filled with nationalist pride or do you identify with global cosmopolitanism?

If Davies is right and our future will take place within this new matrix, I have strong concerns that both sides of the identity divide will gravitate to more collectivist economic strategies, using government when they have power to reward their favored constituencies. Of course, this construct is not set in stone, and will be influenced by external and unanticipated factors.

The Emerging Alignment

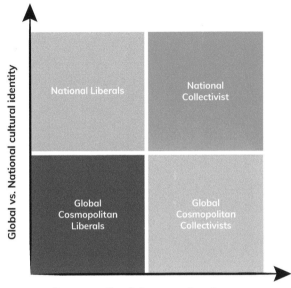

Government's role in economic outcomes

The challenge for those of us in the liberty movement is to envision a new political alignment where we could unite a winning coalition, and then make sure that every issue is seen through the prisms that bring a third framework into focus.

The Future for Which We Should Work

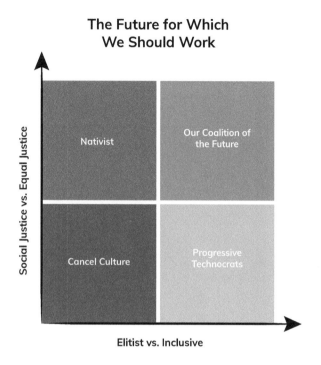

see left liberals like Bill Maher, Matt Taibbi, and Thomas Frank pushing back at the new intolerance. That is progress.

I expect to see more of it, because authentic liberals (and this includes the conservatives and libertarians who also treasure the freedoms in our Founding documents) believe in the dignity of every individual.

People who are unwilling to defend the legal equality of every person are simply not welcome in the coalition I envision. We have no need for those who still harbor the racism that marred America's past, nor the campus radicals who want to silence others' free speech. My envisioned coalition also would not encompass the coastal elites who like to exempt themselves from the rules they wish to impose on those who live in "flyover country."

Every community in our country is full of enterprising people who can solve their own problems if they get a fair shake. When such individuals are able to succeed, they set examples that then are emulated by others. That's how America grew successful. Our task is to prove that that can happen again, and—this time—with *all Americans* invited to share in these blessings of liberty.

If we put our focus on the positive work we can do together, it can melt lingering resentments. The people who committed crimes inside the US Capitol building on January 6, 2021, were *not* representative of the more than seventy million people who cast votes for Donald Trump. The people who set fire to

My suggestion is that we should want those prisms to be those of inclusivity and equal justice for all.

My thinking is that, with respect to the political situation in the United States, (a) Democrats greatly overestimate how many nativist racists exist in Republican ranks and (b) Republicans overestimate the number of Democrats that fit the true "social justice warrior" mold. It is also likely that during the Biden administration the cancel culture types will overstep some bounds and bring a backlash that could split the coalition that voted out President Trump. We already public buildings and looted private businesses during the summer of 2020 were *not* representative of the broader protest movement calling for police reform after the murder of George Floyd.

There is so much bad blood between factions in America's culture wars; I can understand why some will be skeptical about my proposed realignment. They will think I am naive for underestimating the power of the Q'Anon conspiracy theorists within the Republican tribe or the extent to which the Democratic Party has embraced Antifa thugs who (with an irony that's fully lost on them) think you can serve "anti-fascist" goals by employing fascist techniques. I, too, have looked on in horror as those groups have grown, but with clear eyes I believe they remain marginal and are unlikely to gain meaningful cultural power.

I worry most about whether I am overly optimistic about what is in the hearts of the cultural elites who power a large part of the Democratic Party's coalition. They talk a great deal about inclusivity, but the actions of many in this demographic seem emotionally wed to a cultural war that looks down upon heartland Americans with religious values. The way that Big Tech flexed its muscles in early 2021 to deplatform conservative voices on social media suggested that they intend to end the culture war by conquest, rather than finding peace through tolerance and respectful disagreement.

Charles Murray's prescient 2012 book, *Coming Apart*, documented the social bifurca-tion that has replaced the social fluidity that once was embedded in an egalitarian American culture. Our pandemic-era retreat from public spaces and into curated online communities of like-minded individuals has only exacerbated this trend.

We need more interaction with people not like us, not less. Such fluid interaction tends to breed more empathy for the challenges we each grapple with, as well as genuine respect for the know-how and problem-solving strategies that diverse people have developed to get by and to thrive.

In contrast, when we remain isolated in our safe spaces, we tend to become more judgmental about others' situations, or even resentful about their perceived advantages. That creates ripe conditions for demagogues of the political left and political right to sow division and exacerbate, rather than ameliorate, conflicts. They come prepared with a toolbox of pernicious ideas, each of which undermines social harmony and peaceful cooperation and co-existence.

Pernicious Idea #1 — Equality of Outcomes

Our liberal coalition will rally around the idea of equal justice for all. We want everyone to enjoy equal opportunities. We need to go in with a clear-eyed understanding of how that differs from—and is irreconcilable with— mandated equality of outcomes.

Through the progressive lens of social justice, observed inequalities are an affront to the conscience and must be remedied immediately. Social justice warriors approach problems with a moral righteousness that bleeds into arrogance. They have little patience for the liberal mindset; they mistake our cautiousness for callousness.

Through the liberal lens of equal justice, however, the remedies championed by social justice warriors open a Pandora's Box of problems. Once the political class presumes to grant privileges to one group of people and to penalize another, it destroys faith that individuals can expect equal treatment under the law.

Look at the debate over student loan forgiveness, a much-discussed proposal during the campaign season of 2020. Imagine two recent college graduates with $100,000 of debt to repay, and two recent graduates with none. We can easily see that an equality of outcomes can be achieved by changing each person's debt obligation to $50,000, or by eliminating the debt altogether (placing its burden on an abstraction called "the taxpayers"). Does that create justice? What if you learned that one of these individuals in this group graduated debt-free only because she worked several years before and during college to pay her tuition in real time? Doesn't she have reason to resent how the pursuit of equal outcomes resulted in unequal treatment?

Professor David Schmidtz is critical of how modern moral philosophy focuses on the question, "What results are fair?" (about which we have only intuitions) in isolation from the empirically testable question, "What factors produce more beneficial results?" As a metaphor, he discusses a photograph of a busy intersection. If we brush away the responsibility of studying how the traffic system works, we might conclude that it is arbitrary and unjust that "some people have red lights and others have green . . . . In an ideally just world, everyone would have a green light—at the same time. It wouldn't be prosperous. Or productive. Or peaceful. But it would be just."

For this same reason, I believe economist Tomas Piketty's 2015 book, *Capital in the 21st Century*, has had very negative consequences. The book's thesis (summed up with the inequality $r > g$) posited that free enterprise is unfair to its core, because wage growth tends to track with the general growth of the economy (g) whereas investment returns (r) tend to be higher. From that, Piketty concluded that the divide between rich (earning r% on invested capital) and poor (growing their income at g%) will inevitably grow. The thesis remains influential, despite how many times it has been debunked.

This is not the place to fully dissect Piketty's argument, but—in the spirit of Schmidtz's comment above—Piketty's dislike of certain outcomes (wealth inequality) should not excuse him from confronting the fundamental question: how is wealth created in the first place? If we can agree that saving and investment are necessary for innovation and enterprise, it shouldn't be surprising that the risks of investment are rewarded with an expectation of superior returns.

In this way, we look beyond what's visible in a snapshot photo of inequality. We understand observed inequalities are rooted in behavior, opportunities, and institutional arrangements. Where some of us have failed in the past is by being content to simply defend the status quo against ill-considered policy interventions. We need to go deeper. Blanket forgiveness of student loan debt is bad policy, but let's also dig into the reasons why higher education has become unaffordable and why so many graduates are ill-prepared to meet their financial obligations.

Rather than simply proving that Piketty's remedies for addressing wealth inequality will be counterproductive, we need a deeper investigation of whether there are unjust systemic problems that explain data of widening wealth inequalities. Matthew Rognlie famously provides a near-perfect example: then a twenty-six-year-old graduate student, he left a comment at the blog Marginal Revolution which upended Piketty's most dramatic predictions. Rognlie found that the rising inequality Piketty documented could be explained almost entirely by increases in the value of real estate. The implication is that we should be making it easier to develop new housing in high-cost areas, rather than developing new schemes for wealth redistribution.

That is, of course, just the tip of an iceberg of questions we should raise.

Pernicious Idea #2
A Bias for Government Action

In 2003, President George W. Bush summed up what has become conventional wisdom in America and, indeed, much of the world: "When somebody hurts, government has got to move."

That statement is a world away from the wisdom of a different leader, Grover Cleveland, the Democratic president who vetoed a disaster relief bill that aimed to help Texas farmers in 1887. After explaining his view that such a law would be unconstitutional, Cleveland explained why it was also unwise: "The government should not support the people." After all, private charities already had sprung into action in the wake of the disaster. Cleveland went on: "Federal aid in such cases encourages the expectation of paternal care on the part of the government and weakens the sturdiness of our national character, while it prevents the indulgence among our people of that kindly sentiment and conduct which strengthens the bonds of a common brotherhood."

The America that Grover Cleveland describes was largely erased in the course of the twentieth century. No doubt, the people of the United States did great things in the twentieth century, and its government withstood the tests of world wars, economic depression, waves of immigration, and Soviet imperialism.

All that is admirable, but it was accompanied by what the late author and philanthropist Richard Cornuelle described as: "a sustained and continuous transfer of responsibility in a single direction, away from society's most primary institutions—individuals, families, circles of friends, local voluntary organizations, local governments—toward state government and in the end, inevitably, to the federal government."

Cornuelle's article from which this quote is drawn ("De-Nationalizing Community," *Philanthropy*, spring 1996) explains that our civic attachments atrophied as governments stepped in to solve more problems from the top-down. We're left with citizens who no longer feel empowered to solve their own problems; instead, they feel entitled to government-distributed benefits and government solutions to their problems. Communities no longer look after one another because taxpayers figure they are already supporting programs that should address social needs. Mutual aid societies and fraternal organizations once provided voluntary, actuarially sound solutions to the misfortunes and vicissitudes of life. They've vanished and been replaced by promises of our Social Security and Medicare systems—promises that are rather close to running on empty.

Observing American life in the 1830s, Alexis de Tocqueville recognized that local voluntary associations, developed by Americans to solve their own problems independent of government, were essential bulwarks against the systemic weaknesses of democracy. In his treatise, *Democracy in America*, Tocqueville worried that ultimately that decentralized system of problem-solving would be lost to the promises of a paternalist government, enabled by deficit spending. Tocqueville foresaw a soft despotism that "does not break wills, but it softens them, bends them and directs them . . . . Finally it reduces each nation to being nothing more than a flock of timid and industrious animals, of which the government is the shepherd."

Today we sit uncomfortably close to Tocqueville's prediction, with the frontiersman spirit of earlier American history replaced by a promise of "soft spaces" to which one can retreat. Meanwhile, the national debt is more than $80,000 per person, and even that number is dwarfed by the costs of unfunded liabilities within the Medicare and Social Security programs. These entitlement programs are spending more than they take in, and the problem will worsen as the entire Baby Boomer generation will reach retirement age by the end of this decade.

The fiscal recklessness of the US government has been made possible, thus far, by its reserve currency status and the high levels of savings in other parts of the world where dollars are perceived as much more stable than other available options. Will that always be the case?

Part of the liberal agenda in the United States needs to be breaking the addiction to government spending and government actions as the first solutions to our problems, and shifting social problem-solving back to the local level.

Let's add a few words to Bush's statement and turn it on its head: When somebody hurts, government has got to move—that is, *move out of the way*.

Pernicious Idea #3
The Technocratic Illusion

At the heart of our rush to use the blunt instrument of government to achieve our goals, is a final pernicious idea that needs to be confronted by our new liberal coalition. There is an illusion that groups of experts in our capital cities have enough knowledge that we should cede our liberties to their better judgment.

Earlier in this chapter, I made the case that our experience during the pandemic instead proves the opposite. The innovation, resourcefulness, and compassion that we needed came from the bottom up. The costliest mistakes were ones ordered from the top down.

At the end of this chapter, I want to highlight why the instinct to delegate decision-making power to government is not merely opening the door to inefficient outcomes; it is corrosive to a good society. I'll do that with reference to my three favorite "presidential farewells" in American history.

George Washington's Farewell Address is worth reading, even if all you take from it is the elegant prose and self-deprecating humility of America's *Cincinnatus*, but it is also a treasure trove of wisdom. One of the most overlooked sections is about the "spirit of encroachment" that will tempt those with political power to undermine the checks and balances that have been designed to limit their authority. Washington warns citizens to guard the constitutional order and to make sure that changes are adopted lawfully through the Amendment process, not by simple usurpations of powers. Over the past century—with the rise of judicial deference to the administrative state and with the theory of a "living Constitution" subject to convenient reinterpretations by fleeting majorities of the Supreme Court—America has been failing this test.

President Dwight Eisenhower's Farewell Address is remembered for his warning of a rising "military industrial complex," but that was only part of a broader insight concerning the corrupting influence of government funding. Eisenhower saw government incentives having a perverse impact on higher education and scientific research:

> The prospect of domination of the nation's scholars by Federal employment, project allocations, and the power of money is ever present and is gravely to be regarded. Yet, in holding scientific research and discovery in respect, as we should, we must also be alert to the equal and opposite danger that public policy could itself become the captive of a scientific technological elite.

Finally, in President Ronald Reagan's Farewell, he celebrated a resurgence of national pride that he had presided over, but he pressed for "an informed patriotism" without which it would be difficult to preserve American institutions:

> We've got to do a better job of getting across that America is freedom—freedom of speech, freedom of religion, freedom of enterprise. And freedom is special and rare. It's fragile; it needs protection.

The informed patriotism that Reagan called for does not need to gloss over the ugly chapters in American history. The legacy of slavery and discrimination casts a long shadow that deserves a public and honest reckoning. But misguided and ahistorical efforts like *The New York Times'* 1619 Project are harmful to our civil society. We should be able to examine the flaws of our country's Founders without losing sight of their remarkable accomplishments. The toppling of statues in America's towns and cities—initially directed at Confederate generals, but predictably now encompassing the likes of George Washington and Thomas Jefferson—shows an unthinking Jacobin-style radicalism let loose in our culture. That style of revisionist history can be traced back to *avant garde* forms of identity politics, such as critical race theory, that moved out of literature departments and now are colonizing media, entertainment, corporate culture, and government. The trend invites a countermovement, which sadly is prone to manifest itself in a caricature-like white identity politics, and a culture war that only benefits those invested in polarizing our politics.

It is up to us—the freedom movement, and the broad liberal coalition of the future—to put an end to identity politics, and repopularize the enduring historical lessons that come from a country that was "conceived in liberty." Parts of our history are shameful, no doubt, but a fair reading of it can affirm and inspire our commitment to continue moving forward toward justice and social harmony.

When I connect the dots regarding these largely unheeded warnings about threats to the American experiment—politicians ignoring the limits of the authority under the Constitution, the commanding heights of our education establishment beholden to those politicians, and a disingenuous movement to reshape American history around concepts of victimhood—I see the commonsense and good nature of everyday Americans being exploited and their futures being undermined.

It goes without saying that the liberal project is advanced through a search for truth, but that also means holding appropriate skepticism toward those who profess expertise but are conflicted by financial interests or a pre-established narrative.

Big Ideas Along The Path Forward

What could a revival of authentic liberalism accomplish?

- The end of corporate welfare
- A downsizing of Washington DC, relocating major bureaucracies outside the mid-Atlantic corridor
- The end of the drug war and the doctrine of qualified immunity
- Universal education savings accounts to fund students, not schools
- Strengthened protections of First Amendment freedoms and other civil rights enumerated in the Constitution
- A new commitment to global trade
- Restructuring health and welfare systems to incentivize local innovation, and thereby building a better, more responsive safety net

We have very good reason to expect that the above reforms would also move the United States toward other desirable outcomes: a booming economy, a balanced federal budget, greater social mobility, and greater social harmony and toleration by declaring peace in the culture wars.

Down this road, the challenges of our era begin to look small next to the incredible innovations that I hope to see in my remaining years. Among them, the efficiency gains that could come from self-driving cargo transport, the widespread use of blockchain to decentralize commerce and culture, an explosion of virtual reality-based entertainment, interplanetary travel, and anti-aging technologies. (And if the last comes online in time, I might hope that my number of remaining years will tick upwards rather dramatically.)

The possibilities in front of us are awe inspiring. So *why not* think big about a coming renaissance in liberal reform?

I am thrilled that so many inspiring organizations—in the United States and around the world—have partnered through Atlas Network to plant important seeds of change.

In Part 1 of this book, I presented some of the freedom movement's biggest accomplishments of the past ten years, as well as photos from inside the trenches of ongoing work with our partners. I want to conclude this final chapter by returning again to some of the inspiring stories I hear from partners in the freedom movement on a regular basis.

- I'm always amazed when I see brand new organizations achieve meaningful policy impact. Such is the case with Montana's Frontier Institute, which was created in 2020 but is already seeing its Montana Recovery Agenda serving as a road map as the state's new governor cuts red tape that unnecessarily slows the state's economy.

- Similarly, I have high hopes for the Better Cities Project, which was founded in 2019. A major focus is reforming exclusionary zoning laws, which had racist goals when they were implemented broadly in the United States one hundred years ago, and which continue to visit disproportionate harm on minority and low-income communities today.

o Another young organization, Free The People, has landed Netflix distribution for some of their films, including an inspiring documentary, *How to Love Your Enemies*, about "restorative justice"—an innovative alternative to the traditional criminal justice system that's yielding exciting results in Longmont, Colorado.

o The Property and Environment Research Center (PERC), founded in 1980 in Bozeman, Montana, deserves credit for changing conventional wisdom on a topic—environmental conservation—that some believe can only be tackled by government intervention. Recently, PERC solved a population crisis among wild horses in the American West by advancing a reform to incentivize private adoption. The result: more humane outcomes for horses and more savings for taxpayers by avoiding the need for government-run facilities.

o Another innovative Atlas Network partner—the Foundation for Individual Rights in Education in Philadelphia,

Pennsylvania—is protecting freedom of speech and other fundamental rights in American universities and colleges, and doing so regardless of the content or political persuasions of the censored speakers.

o To our south, the Fundación Eléutera in Honduras has been active in the process of liberating that nation's energy sector from government monopoly, with the goal of giving access to electricity to more Hondurans at lower cost. In Uruguay, Atlas Network partners such as Centro de Estudios para el Desarrollo mobilized public demand for more limited government, which saw the baseline federal budget decline in 2020 to save taxpayers approximately $660 million annually.

o In Africa, the Centre for Development and Enterprises–Great Lakes (CDE) ran a campaign called "Birashoboka!" ("It's Possible") to improve the climate for business in Burundi, which ranked near the bottom of the world on such measures. CDE's efforts catalyzed a 72 percent reduction in the time it took to start a business; new business registrations in Burundi leapt by 49 percent in the wake of those reforms. In Côte d'Ivoire (Ivory Coast), the Audace Institut Afrique developed an exciting methodology, working with traditional communal structures and using GPS and smartphone technologies, to establish secure property titles and reliable village land registers. Providing secure property rights liberates people to realize the value of their assets and diminishes the likelihood of conflict over property boundaries.

- In Sri Lanka, Advocata Institute led a charge against punitive taxes on feminine sanitary products, which were at a level—over 100 percent—that made a basic necessity unaffordable for most women in the country. With prices dramatically lowered, more women can spend more time in school and in the workplace than was possible in the past. In central Asia, the brave team of the Afghanistan Economic and Legal Studies Organization promotes entrepreneurship, human rights, and religious tolerance via the thirty-nine radio programs (in Dari, Pashto, and English) of its Silk Road Station.

- In the UK, the Institute of Economic Affairs in London has effectively advocated for free trade deals in the wake of Brexit. The free trade push has already resulted in sixty-three such deals, covering trade of about £885 billion. In Serbia, a young group called Libek created an online media outlet, "Talas" ("The Wave" in Serbian), that shares classical liberal ideas, analyses, and commentary with more than twenty million people in the Balkans.

As you can see, amid the many challenges to freedom in 2021, positive change *is* possible. It's happening. It's also time to do more.

Let's return to the question I asked in the Introduction. Is the sun of liberalism rising or setting?

I hope the pages of this volume have persuaded you to reject the pessimism so many feel and instead see the great opportunities for liberalism and the free society before us. The opportunities are there, waiting for the freedom movement to make our move.

No doubt, there will be setbacks on the path forward. But I reject the idea that the future is bound to be less free than today. I reject pessimism for a simple reason: it tends to be self-fulfilling. The future belongs to optimists.

When I look around the world, I see that the "twenty-first century socialism" that was so fashionable a decade ago under Hugo Chavez has been smashed against the shores of reality in Venezuela. Once again, socialism has drowned those who were forced on board.

I see cracks in the Chinese model that are bound to grow over time.

I see political Islamism receding with the memories of the stone-age depravities we saw undertaken by the monstrous killers of

ISIS five years ago. More temperate voices are showing how religion can be reconciled with modernity.

In Africa, members of young generations have windows to the world that were once unavailable; and they are increasingly standing up against the corrupt government, political violence, bureaucratic arrogance, and cronyism that has slowed the pace of enterprise in the past.

This year—2021—is a year for optimism about the future. It is a time for courage and boldness among all those who love liberty, peace, and hope. Our strategies—for removing barriers to opportunity, and unleashing the creative capacities of free people—have worked in the past, and will work again. We should demonstrate the confidence of our convictions.

The future belongs to those who embrace reason, civility, and opportunity, and not to those who seek to silence others and to sow division in our societies.

The future belongs to the advocates of authentic liberalism—open and entrepreneurial, inclusive and generous. We seek no end-state Utopia, but we know that it's through the iterative innovations of free people that societies will continue to enjoy improving standards of living and more opportunities to pursue happiness.

It's an inspiring vision, isn't it? Together we can make it come true.

Thank You

I am incredibly fortunate to work among colleagues who keep me learning all the time. Those who spent extra hours with me on chapters of this book include Tom Palmer, Matt Warner, A.J. Skiera, and—in particular—Lisa Conyers who copiloted this project to its destination. Big thanks as well to Dara Ekanger for her elegant copyediting and Colleen Cummings for her fantastic graphic design.

Roberto Salinas-León made a crucial contribution in introducing me to Carlos Newland and Pál Czeglédi; the result is the Global Index for Market Mentality, summarized in Chapter 5 and to be presented more formally in the Fall 2021 issue of *Cato Journal.*

The book is also shaped by conversations over the years with thousands of Atlas Network friends and benefactors. I especially treasure insights that I learned from two value investors turned philanthropists, the late Sir John Templeton and the late Don Smith. Indeed, the John Templeton Foundation and Smith Family Foundation made possible the photojournalism that is presented in Chapter 3.

Also, this book would not exist if not for Nicolás Ibáñez Scott's encouragement to confront difficult questions and take a sober assessment of why liberalism is visibly declining in so many places. I also want to thank the Lynde and Harry Bradley Foundation for an invitation that inspired me to develop ideas in Chapter 12, as well as the anonymous donors behind our Rainbow@Atlas fund who helped me appreciate how we need to be more proactive in showing how *equality* and *inclusivity* are at the heart of the movement we are building.

I owe a debt of gratitude to the participants in the regional discussions that are transcribed in Chapters 6-11. I'm privileged to have so many warmhearted and thoughtful friends all over the globe!

I also am grateful to have parents and siblings (and uncles too) who taught me to appreciate the blessings of free societies. And, finally, a thank you to my wife, Stephanie, and the kids—for making sure the *pursuit of happiness* is not an abstract concept in my life, but a practical task for us to take on, together, every day.

About the Author

Brad Lips joined Atlas Network in 1998 and became its CEO in 2009. He's proud to have seen this non-profit organization—dedicated to securing, for all individuals, the rights to economic and personal liberty—grow in dramatic ways over the past decade.

Brad struggles to connect the dots among his pre-Atlas Network career, but here goes . . . . Brad's Princeton thesis on rap music and his adventures in indie rock journalism taught him that there's nothing as exciting as individual creativity, especially when it disrupts old ideas and conventions. Brad's involvement in online businesses during the dawn of the commercial internet exposed him to the power of online communities and the courage required of entrepreneurs. His stint on Wall Street educated him on the power and efficiency of free capital markets, but also the difficulty of aligning incentives in any large and complex institution.

He was drawn to the think tank space because of his sincere belief in the morality of free enterprise and liberal institutions, and his concern about their fragility. For a time, he worried that very few others would ever understand why his career felt like a "moral calling." When he arrived at Atlas Network, however, he discovered there were awe-inspiring efforts to overcome different types of tyranny all over the world, and he realized these projects needed to be shared more broadly.

Brad and his wife have been privileged to get to know many of these heroes of the freedom movement and host them in their home — with grand hopes that the kids in the house also will find inspiration in their brave examples!

As *Liberalism and the Free Society in 2021* goes to print, Brad is excited that a growing number of people of different stripes are discovering the work of Atlas Network's partners in the U.S. and worldwide.

About Atlas Network

Atlas Network is a non-profit organization, based in Arlington, Virginia, that aims to secure for all individuals the rights to economic and personal freedom.

Founded in 1981 by think tank pioneer Sir Antony Fisher, Atlas Network has a global vision of a free, prosperous, and peaceful world where the principles of individual liberty, property rights, limited government, and free markets are secured by the rule of law.

Atlas Network's vision is best achieved by independent think tanks with the local knowledge to be effective agents of change, prioritizing institutional increases in freedom that can improve opportunities for vast numbers of people.

To accelerate the pace of achievement by its partners in their communities, Atlas Network implements programs within its Coach, Compete, Celebrate™ strategic model.

Atlas Network is not endowed and accepts no government funding. It depends on private philanthropy to carry out its annual programs, which includes awarding seed funding for more than one hundred of the most promising projects developed by its partners.

Learn about how you can get involved at AtlasNetwork.org.

CPSIA information can be obtained
at www.ICGtesting.com
Printed in the USA
BVHW020433280721
612697BV00002BA/3